Housing Costs and Housing Needs

edited by
Alexander Greendale
Stanley F. Knock, Jr.

The Praeger Special Studies program—
utilizing the most modern and efficient book
production techniques and a selective
worldwide distribution network—makes
available to the academic, government, and
business communities significant, timely
research in U.S. and international economic, social, and political development.

Housing Costs and Housing Needs

PRAEGER SPECIAL STUDIES IN U.S. ECONOMIC, SOCIAL, AND POLITICAL ISSUES

Praeger Publishers   New York   Washington   London

Library of Congress Cataloging in Publication Data
Main entry under title:

Housing costs and housing needs.

  (Praeger special studies in U.S. economic, social, and
political issues)
  √ 1. Housing policy—United States—Addresses, essays,
lectures. √2. Housing—United States—Addresses, essays,
lectures. √I. Greendale, Alexander. √II. Knock, Stanley F.
HD7293.H583   301.5'4'0973   75-26107
ISBN 0-275-56220-4

301. 5
H 84

mN

Papers delivered at a conference entitled
"Decent Housing: A Promise to Keep"
(April 22-24, 1975, Washington, D.C.).
Sponsored by the Interreligious Coalition
for Housing. Included is a follow-up
Action Guide based on the papers and proceedings.

PRAEGER PUBLISHERS
111 Fourth Avenue, New York, N.Y. 10003, U.S.A.

Published in the United States of America in 1976
by Praeger Publishers, Inc.

All rights reserved

© 1976 by Praeger Publishers, Inc.

Printed in the United States of America

PREFACE

The Interreligious Coalition for Housing (ICH) comprises Protestant, Catholic, and Jewish groups working toward the fulfillment of the promise "a decent home for all," as adopted by Congress in the National Housing Act of 1949 and reaffirmed in 1968 and again in 1974. Operating from the common understanding that religious groups should be instruments of creative solutions to human problems, the coalition strives for the following:

To reorder our national priorities and resources to provide adequate housing programs, especially for the poor and low- and moderate-income families, as well as for the elderly, the handicapped, and single adults;

To create among religious, government, labor, banking, business, and professional people a new consciousness that housing can be a tool to enable people to live fuller lives;

To enable religious and community groups to develop effective housing models that meet local and regional needs;

To provide housing consumers with information, education and training systems, technical assistance, and management consultative services.

ICH has built or been otherwise directly involved in the creation of approximately 100,000 units of housing for families, singles, the elderly, and the handicapped in urban, suburban, and rural areas. Developments have included federal programs 231, 221(d)(3), 235, 236, and leasing Section 23, in both new and rehabilitated units. These 100,000 units make up more than half of the nonprofit housing built, with a failure rate of less than 6 percent—surely an enviable record.

The ICH conference on Housing held in Washington, D.C., on April 22-24, 1975, brought together close to 450 participants from every section of the country, many of them experts in the housing field. They came to evaluate the devastating effect that the state of the economy and the federal housing subsidy moratorium has had on the housing construction industry, to address themselves to the needs of the close to 80 percent of all Americans who have been priced out of the housing market, and to examine how the 1974 Housing and Community Development Act might counteract these bleak facts and help turn housing around. The papers presented were prepared with these concerns in mind.

HUNT LIBRARY
CARNEGIE-MELLON UNIVERSITY
PITTSBURGH, PENNSYLVANIA 15213

JUN 24 '77

It was recognized at the conference that the executive branch of the federal government has embraced the "trickle-down theory," by which the poor and low-income people are expected to follow the free enterprise pattern of seeking to meet their housing needs on the "open market" of private industry (financing, construction, rental), and should not expect to become homeowners until they have proved themselves economically stable enough to support the requirements of private moneylenders.

In contrast, the legislative branch of the federal government is steadfastly opposed to the trickle-down theory as a basis for housing the nation's poor and low-income people and to the proposition that economic stability on the terms of the moneylending industry is an absolute precondition for property ownership. Therefore, it passes laws enacting programs based upon different assumptions, it funds these laws, and it goes to court to enforce its legislation and the authorization of funds, but it fails to override vetoes and thus creates confusion for everyone in the housing field.

Yet there are opportunities. Those desirous of fulfilling the housing commitment will have to examine each situation with precision, extreme accuracy, and a well-informed knowledge of the effective limits of the various tools available. When such hard-nosed feasibility studies indicate genuine potential for accomplishing the goal of decent housing for the poor and low- and moderate-income people, then action can and should be taken.

Beyond the basic problems relating to the production of new housing units to replace those demolished for whatever the reason and to accommodate the increase in net population and the shifting of family size and life styles, there are areas—as outlined in our Action Guide—in which those committed to decent housing can make meaningful contributions. These contributions will have the net effect of keeping existing housing from getting worse and improving the length of time existing housing remains in the housing market, thereby generally reducing the pressures building up in our society for better housing.

The Housing and Community Development Act of 1974 contains major provisions for local communities to develop housing plans in order to obtain their community development block grants. Much can and needs to be done to ensure that these provisions are met in a way that serves the needs of poor people as well as others. Even more can and needs to be done to ensure that the block grant funds are, in fact, used appropriately.

In summary, although the housing situation looks bleak from many valid viewpoints, there are avenues for those who desire to make a meaningful contribution to providing housing for all citizens. Even though national leadership is confused and contradictory, there are many opportunities to maintain significant output in, and support of, meeting housing needs at the local, community level for those who are willing to do the hard work it requires.

In the words of the Reverend Nicholas Hood, president pro tem. of the Detroit City Council, in addressing the ICH participants:

> The 1949, 1968 and 1974 Housing Acts promised a decent home for all, but this promise is yet to be fulfilled. This promise can only be kept if the Federal Government makes the commitment to housing that is in the language of these Acts. This promise can be kept if we of the Interreligious Coalition can get Congress to adopt those housing programs which we know will work.

The conference served to reawaken and give direction to a new national drive directed to housing needs for which subsidy costs must be found. Our Action Guide, based on the papers and proceedings of the conference, points to some new as well as some established approaches. No organization in the country has the resources available to ICH. The coalition intends to make full use of these resources so that the promise of decent housing for all Americans will be a promise and covenant that is kept.

CONTENTS

PART II: ACTION GUIDE

       The Current Situation   69
       Opportunities for Advocacy   70
       Housing Needs in Your Community   70
       Housing Subsidies in Your Community   71
       Community Development Programs   72
       Section 8 Housing Assistance Program   72
       Growth and Access to Land   72
       Civil Rights   73
       Federal Legislation   73
       State Legislation   74

2   DEVELOPMENT   75

       Introduction   75
       Communicating the Need   75
       Obtaining Parent-Body Approval   76
       How Much Will It Cost?   78
       The Organizing Committee   81
       The Consultant   81
       The Attorney   82
       The Housing Market Analysis   83
       Site Selection   88
       The Professional Real Estate Agent   89
       The Development Team   91
       The Economic Feasibility Study   94
       Sections 8 and 202 Programs   95
       Finding New Ways to Finance Housing   102
       The Application Process   106
       Construction   112
       Management   113
       Rural Housing Development   114
       Federal Programs and Resources for Rural Housing
           Needs   116
       FmHA and How It Operates   123
       Financial and Technical Assistance Resources   124
       Servicing the Project   127

LIST OF FIGURES

(Condensed from the Keynote Address by the Right
Reverend Paul Moore, Jr., Bishop of New York
[Episcopal])

Whenever I find myself in Washington, looking out at many familiar faces, I get a sense of deja vu. Over the years we have come down here again and again for civil rights, for home rule for the District of Columbia, on behalf of Resurrection City, for the march for peace, for amnesty, to try to prevent the energy crisis from hurting the poor—and now we come for housing.

There are those who say we churchmen scatter our shots. But scatter our shots we must to seek to elicit concern for basic human need in whatever form, so that we may be witness to the gospel demand in an increasingly complex society.

Today we turn to housing: first, to meet a basic human need; second, to defend the poor against the principalities and powers of our system that systematically lay waste acres and acres of housing; and third, to seek to rebuild our cities for a more mystic reason—so that the great image of the city will be lifted up before the eyes of man. The city is the place on earth where varied multitudes seek out the destiny of living their lives in total dependence, one on the other. The city is the source of civilization's creative dynamism. Granted, the city has fostered and shown forth the dark underside of human nature. Nevertheless, it continues to be the only model we have in which we all must believe. The Lord demands that we live together and that our destiny be, and always be, with our neighbor. As different wounds in the body politic appear and as different social dynamics sweep across the world, the human spirit responds in different ways, and we who are a Bible people seek God's will for us in a given historical moment.

In the 1950s, the war was over and we were involved in rebuilding America in a new way. The country, through its postwar housing program, invested in the illusory Eden of suburbia. Never having really understood what makes a city, under the rubric of the Wagner-Ellender-Taft Bill, we bulldozed huge fields of human communities. Was it not a massive, obscene revelation of the national subconscious that the high-rise public housing of the 1950s resembled prisons and mental hospitals? Did no one realize the impossibility of building a community around an elevator shaft and a patch of grass 20 feet below?

In the 1960s, the time of massive social unrest and movement, neighborhoods of people insisted on being involved in housing, and there was the beginning of operating subsidies for low-cost housing. The 235-236 programs, with a mixture of private and public initiatives, failed to effectively reach the poor because they lacked a heavy enough public subsidy.

The 1970s saw new experimentation aimed at flexibility with such programs as "turn-key," but again, these programs lacked sufficient depth and quantity. Then came the complete federal freeze on housing in 1973.

What is the Church's mission today? As I see it, it is to teach the truth about housing, to help build communities, and to renew the importance of the city in the life of America. The Church should help set guidelines for human housing, encouraging low-rise houses, rehabilitation that preserves neighborhoods, scatter-site housing, small units, and tenant ownership. The Church should be a catalyst for community building. We must be like the wise man who builds his house upon the rock. Over the years, we have not built our houses solidly upon the rock of human community, and so they have literally fallen down or been torn down, like the infamous Igoe-Pruitt housing project in St. Louis.

In recent years, neighborhood groups have sprung up with strong leadership, vigor, and a good deal of know-how. They have formed effective coalitions for realistic rehabilitation of housing. It is the Church's vocation to support such groups, which stress rehabilitation and ownership of housing by the poor, either by sweat equity or by a one-time write-down on the cost of rehabilitation. In the long run, these are the cheapest possible ways of subsidizing housing. In a sense, it is conservative in ideology, for it winds up with homeownership and is a dignified way for people to live. Perhaps the 1974 Housing and Community Development Act can be of help in this effort.

Finally, we must continue to see housing as only one of the interdependent urban problems. On the positive side, a strong federal housing program will generate a great deal of employment. We know, however, that good housing by itself is useless unless there are also jobs and decent transportation.

Let us once again emphasize that the destiny of Western civilization still coincides with the destiny of the metropolis and that the segregation of our neighborhoods caused by bad housing policy affects the education, the employment, and the very economic and political stability of the metropolis. We ask the Holy Spirit tonight to empower us that we may take up once again the cause of housing for the poor and the near-poor. As in Matthew 7:24: "Everyone, then, who hears these words of mine and does them will be like a wise man who builds his house upon the rock."

(Condensed from the Remarks by Senator
Harrison A. Williams, Jr., of New Jersey)

Congress worked very hard last year to pass a comprehensive
housing bill. I am proud to say that I fought for language to be included
in the bill to revitablize the Section 202 housing program for the elderly.
The signing of the Housing and Community Development Act on August
22, 1974, was a happy event for me and for thousands of concerned
Americans who have been fighting for a senior citizen housing program
over the years.

It is the congressional intent that the revised 202 program be
used in tandem with the new Section 8 program. In that way, no tenant
would be required to pay more than 25 percent of his income for rent.
Through this revised program, I think we can preserve the advantages
of the original 202 program and at the same time provide greater rental assistance to older Americans, including those in the very lowest
range of income.

There should be no question in anyone's mind about the need
for this program. There are hundreds of thousands of elderly persons
on waiting lists to get into housing—good housing, similar to the kind
many of you stand proudly behind. There are hundreds of dedicated,
experienced, committed, and energetic nonprofit sponsors in every
state of the country anxious and eager to put their reputations on the
line for decent housing for the elderly. What's more, most of these
organizations have already demonstrated that they are equal to the
challenge. It is heartwarming to me that there are so many organizations ready and willing to build—and, more important, to maintain—
good senior citizen housing.

As chairman of the Subcommittee on Housing for the Elderly;
as a member of the Senate Housing, Banking, and Urban Affairs Committee, which drafted the bill; and as one of the Senate conferees who
met with our counterparts from the House to iron out our differences,
I have a pretty good idea of what we intended. At no time did we intend to change the long-standing focus of Section 202 on providing
funds for permanent financing. Anyone with the slightest degree of
experience in the field of housing for the elderly knows that the major
obstacle facing the nonprofit sponsor is permanent financing. You
just cannot get it without some governmental program to assist you.
The intent of Congress in revising the 202 program was to provide
permanent financing—not construction loans.

Using 202 funds for construction loans is not necessarily a bad
idea—as long as permanent financing is readily available as well.
For example, it is possible for the administration to allow the Government National Mortgage Association (GNMA-Ginny Mae) to buy out
the 202 loans. This might very well encourage the major lenders to

provide sufficient permanent financing for nonprofit sponsors. Such an arrangement could allow 202 loans to be called in once a project was constructed and rented. Then the money could be loaned out again so that many more units could be built. I believe this approach has great promise.

You may be sure that I will not relax my efforts. For one thing, I will soon be reissuing a questionnaire I circulated two years ago in which I asked each 202 project sponsor how long his waiting list was. Certainly, this is an imperfect measurement of the true need for housing, but at least it gives some indication. The results of the last survey received a great deal of attention and helped to underscore the need for a dynamic 202 program.

Second, I have asked the staff of the Subcommittee on Housing for the Elderly to work closely with the Appropriations Committee. I am determined that the level of approval for Section 202 be increased.

I do not have to tell you that the stumbling block is not, and never has been, the Congress. There is widespread recognition, in both the House and the Senate and among both Democrats and Republicans, of the need to provide much greater support for housing for the elderly. That is why we were able to fashion a revised and revitalized 202 program. But we have had to battle the administration for every inch of ground we gained, and we are still battling today. Together, we hope, we can get the message across to the administration.

(Condensed from the Remarks of Representative
Parren Mitchell of Maryland)

In the more than four years that I have been in the Congress and moving around this country, I have tried my best to translate to the various audiences to which I have spoken something of the pain that I was enduring because I would see program after program—parts of the Great Society—eroded and destroyed. I knew that when we put the Legal Services Program of the Office of Economic Opportunity (OEO) into a bureaucratic strait jacket, poor and oppressed people would not have a vehicle to help them. I knew that the moratorium placed on housing funds meant that those who were black most often had to pay a "black tax," that is, an extra margin of profit derived from the rent or the purchase of a home, which still exists, despite civil rights laws. Most painful was not seeing the troops that had been there in 1954, 1956, and 1958 fighting for the poor and wondering what happened to them.

This is why being with you here today is so enjoyable. From all over the nation, you have come to renew this commitment. I am grateful to you for endorsing the housing bill I introduced. We will need all the help we can get in getting that bill passed. There is resistance against doing anything more for "those people" because of our huge budgetary deficit.

Franklin Roosevelt talked about seeing one-third of the nation ill-housed, ill-clothed, and ill-fed, yet in 1975 we see 14.5 million households in America with incomes of less than $5,000 living in unsafe, unsanitary housing that they cannot even afford. We need you to be the advocates for these people.

I am a proud man and do not like to beg. But I beg you to address yourself to the whole panorama of pathologies and ills that are affecting those in our communities who can least afford to cope with a system not designed for their betterment. I beg you not to succumb to phrases such as that of A. E. Housman: "How am I to face the odds of man's bedevilment and God's? I am strangely afraid of the world I never made." Rather, help me, help them, and help ourselves and yourselves!

(Excerpts from the Remarks by Representative
Edward I. Koch of New York)

There is a housing crisis in America today—one that the administration seems to care little about but which exists nonetheless.

Library of Congress figures show over 13 million families living in "deprivation" in the United States, which means inadequate plumbing and other utilities, rent too high for the family's means, too little space for the number of people, and so on. Housing construction and home purchasing is at an all-time low, and mortgage foreclosures are at an all-time high. The recession has hit the construction industry probably harder than any other segment of the economy.

These grim facts have moved the Congress to take some action. Rebates of up to $2,000 for the purchase of a private home is provided by the tax rebate bill, which is now public law. The House has passed and sent to the Senate the Emergency Middle Income Housing Act, providing for 6 and 7 percent mortgages for the purchase of private homes, condominiums, and coops. Finally, the House has passed and sent to the Senate the Emergency Homeowners Relief Act, providing monthly mortgage payments of up to $250 if the homeowner is threatened with eviction because of economic conditions.

While I hope that these bills providing assistance to the private homeowner will be enacted, what of the one-third of the nation that rents its homes or apartments? New York City is 63 percent renter and 37 percent owner. Of the 2.8 million housing units in New York, 2.2 million are rental. In the District of Columbia, there are 3,000-4,000 tenant evictions a year because of nonpayment, and the National Tenants' Organization reports similar figures for other cities.

I am delighted that the Senate Banking Committee has agreed to include an amendment to the Emergency Housing Act, on the floor today, which I had supported in the House, to include Ginny Mae assistance to multifamily units. I am hopeful that the full Senate will accept this provision and that the conferees will keep it. In New York City one year ago, there was only one Federal Housing Administration (FHA) unsubsidized multifamily project in default. Today there are 26.

But I am also hopeful that, while we need to assist multifamily developers and building owners, we must also assist the tenants who are being evicted. Whether you live in an apartment or a private house and whether you own your home and pay a mortgage or rent your home and pay a landlord, your home is your home, and an eviction is the same whether you rent or own. Congress must address this problem, and I will work to see that it does.

The Congress must address another critical problem—the over-institutionalization and the removal from their homes of our elderly and disabled. Many elderly and disabled persons are forced from their own homes into hospitals or nursing homes because of the lack of reasonable alternatives. A January 1975 Health, Education, and Welfare (HEW) study stated that as many as 144,000-260,000—or 14 to 26 percent of the nation's one million nursing home patients—may be being "unnecessarily maintained in an institutional environment."

It is incongrous that, because of a lack of alternatives and because our medicare and medicaid laws cover far more institutionalization than home health care, we are legally and financially forcing the institutionalization of our elderly. Virtually every elderly person entering a nursing home does so with sadness, fearing that this move will be his or her last.

There is a major loophole in the law in that part-time care at home, for those who do not require the full range of services of a nursing home, is far cheaper: estimates by the General Accounting Office (GAO), the Library of Congress, and others indicate that it is about one-third the cost of nursing homes. If they are able, patients should at least be able to choose which they prefer—an option that would cost the government less per patient.

With 84 House sponsors to date, and with Senator Moss, chairman of the Senate Subcommittee on Long Term Care, and five others introducing the bill on the Senate side, I have introduced the National Home Health Care Act of 1975 (H.R. 4772 and S. 1163), after meeting with, and inviting the comments of, 269 organizations. This bill provides unlimited visiting nurse and doctor visits, as needed, to avoid institutionalization; supportive services, such as transportation, shopping, and walking assistance; and rent subsidies or private home mortgage and repair cost subsidies. The amount of rent would be the fraction of the household that the elderly or disabled person represents, up to the amount already fixed by Housing and Urban Development (HUD) for federally assisted housing. If the individual chooses to own his own home, the payments would be the same as if he were eligible under HUD rental assistance.

The National Home Health Care Act also authorizes the secretary of HUD to expand the congregate housing program (Section 315) that Senator Cranston and I successfully included in the 1974 Housing and Community Development Act.

The bill is now before the House Ways and Means Subcommittee on Health, chaired by Representative Daniel Rostenkowski, and the House Interstate and Foreign Commerce Subcommittee on Health and the Environment, chaired by Representative Paul Rogers. In the Senate, the bill is before the Finance Committee. I hope these committees will take prompt action on this critical legislation, which allows those elderly and disabled who do not require the full range of services of a nursing home to live in their own homes.

(Condensed from the Remarks of Representative
Andrew Young of Georgia)

It is a pleasure to be here and to see so many good friends. I would like to remind you where you came from and how you got here and see if we can get some sense of direction about the future.

We were a part of a movement that made for great changes in this nation. Every president who moved to do something of significance for people responded only when confronted by a mass movement. Many of you were a part of religious delegations that went in the early 1960s to talk with John Kennedy about civil rights legislation and years later to talk with Lyndon Johnson about voting rights. The point I make is that nothing happens unless people at the grass roots level force it to happen. Bureaucratic and political inertia does not respond until there is a crisis and an emergency. It is just a question of whether the crisis is going to be expressed in a chaotic and discordant manner or in an organized manner that brings about positive and creative change.

What is needed in our society is the stabilization of our economy. A major expenditure in housing construction will put people back to work, which will contribute to more tax dollars, which will help us to deal with the deficit. Every billion dollars of expanded gross national product brings in about $350 million of federal, state, and local taxes. One reason we have a federal deficit is not that the government is spending too much but that it is spending on items that are not productive for an expanding, growing economy. When you build a Trident submarine that goes out into the middle of the sea and goes to the bottom, only one group of people shares those dollars. When you build housing, those dollars continue to cycle through the economy, where they are taxed over and over again and bring about creative and constructive economic growth.

We are going to have to decide which side we are on and act forthright and with nerve! HUD would prefer not to foreclose on many of its deteriorating properties. With the rents available, why don't people and groups get contracts to get the necessary work done on these properties and then leave to Congress the financial takeovers!

It is time somebody said, "Everybody has the right to a house or an apartment, and, whatever money is available in our community, we are going to use it to provide such housing if the government does not." The government eventually must and will get back into housing. But unless we are willing to become part of a housing movement that forces the government to be responsive to the people's housing needs, we compound the problem by avoiding it.

CONFERENCE COSPONSORS

American Federation of Labor-Congress of Industrial Organizations

American Institute of Architects

American Jewish Committee's National Job-Linked-Housing Center

Center for Community Change

Commission on Regional and Local Ecumenism

Connecticut Interfaith Housing

Health, Education, and Welfare Association, United Presbyterian Church

Housing Assistance Council

Interreligious New Communities Coalition

League of Women Voters

Los Angeles Interfaith Community Housing

Michigan Committee on Law and Housing

National Association for the Advancement of Colored People

National Association of Home Builders

National Association of Housing and Redevelopment Officials

National Committee Against Discrimination in Housing

National Housing and Human Development Alliance

National Housing Services

National Interfaith Coalition on Aging

National Rural Housing Coalition

National Tenants Organization

National Urban League

Rural Housing Alliance

United Auto Workers of America

United Mine Workers of America

CONFERENCE PARTICIPANTS

Thomas Muller is the Director of Evaluation Studies of the Urban Institute's Land Use Center. He was a Professorial Lecturer at the American University and Head of Management Systems Projects, Washington Office, System Development Corporation. He has written extensively on project management, research techniques, fiscal and land use analyses, feasibility studies, public school finance, land development, population, and metropolitan growth.

Sherman Joseph Maisel is Professor of Business Administration at the University of California, Berkeley. He was on the Board of Governors of the Federal Reserve System; a foreign service economist with the U.S. Department of State; a fellow of the Center for Advanced Studies in Behavioral Sciences; a member of the advisory committees to the Bureau of Census and the National Bureau of Economic Research; a trustee of the Population Reference Bureau; and past president of the American Finance Association. He is the author of Housebuilding in Transition (1953), Fluctuations, Growth and Forecasting (1957), Financing Real Estate (1965), and Managing the Dollar (1973).

George Sternlieb is Director of the Center for Urban Policy Research at Rutgers University. He was cofounder of EDP and its offshoot, Keydata, which pioneered in on-line data processing service; past chairman and current member of the Census Advisory Committee on Small Areas; Director, Citizens Housing and Planning Council; Director, New Community Development Foundation, Inc.; a member of the Federal Rent Advisory Board (1973) and the Presidential Task Force on Housing (1972); and currently serves as a member of the National Institute of Mental Health. He is on the Editorial Advisory Board of New York Affairs, Policy and Politics, Real Estate Law Journal, and Urban Affairs Quarterly. He has been a consultant to cities, states, the federal government, and numerous agencies. His articles and books have given him an international reputation, and he is considered one of the world's leading "think-tankers" in the field of housing.

David Listokin is a Research Associate at the Center for Urban Policy Research at Rutgers University. His writings include The Dynamics of Housing Rehabilitation, Funding Education, and The Environmental Impact Handbook (with Richard Burchell).

William D. Hughes is Director of Education and Training, American Association of Homes for the Aging. He was Chief of Elderly Housing Assistance, HUD; Director of Elderly Housing Loans, HUD; and Housing Management Coordinator and Chief of Project Fiscal Management and Program Budgets of the U.S. Public Housing Authority.

Cushing Dolbeare is a Consultant on Housing Policy for the National Tenants Organization. She has served as Managing Director of the Housing Association of Delaware Valley; Assistant Director of the Philadelphia Housing Association; a consultant to the American Friends Service Committee; and the Executive Director of the National Rural Housing Coalition and Rural Housing Information Service. She has written extensively on housing.

William Brauer is the President of National Realty Advisors and the Managing Director of Medical Facilities Consultants. He is a member of the Institute of Real Estate Management and a Fellow of the Royal Society of Health (Great Britain). He has over 28 years of experience in development, management, and counseling related to real estate and physical facilities for profit and nonprofit use. He is a nationally recognized lecturer on real estate development, market analyses, and taxation as it relates to real estate development and utilization.

PART

I

ISSUES AND PROPOSALS

1

ISSUES IN
LAND USE POLICIES
AND HOUSING

INTRODUCTION

Many land use and adequate housing issues are closely interrelated. The construction of additional housing units outside developed urban core areas generally requires that existing land uses—usually open space—be changed to somewhat more intensive development. The absence of new construction creates additional pressure on low- and moderate-income households, which are at the end of the housing chain.

New housing on the periphery of urbanized areas, where much of it is concentrated, frequently conflicts with land use policies or objectives aimed at reducing urban sprawl. In the absence of any existing or anticipated strong state or federal guidelines, it is local government that determines, in most cases, the location and type of new residential housing.*

Many land use issues are of only secondary interest to those directly concerned with expanding the supply of low- and moderate-income housing, since new developments—particularly detached units —are usually aimed at an above-average household income market.

It is important to recognize that, on the average, new construction adds only 2 percent to our total housing stock annually. Since new units, other than mobile homes, tend to be more expensive than the existing housing stock, only a small number of low- and moderate-

---

*This view differs from that of those who anticipate that states or federal agencies will take an active role in land use policies. The resistance is sufficiently strong to inhibit a meaningful nonlocal land use role in residential housing.

income households can be provided with decent new housing in the absence of large-scale government aid.* As a result, moderate-income households benefit from new construction primarily because it vacates older housing, usually at the urban core and inner suburbs.

Since 1974 there has been a dramatic reduction in new housing starts. The political and environmental pressures for land use legislation at the local, state, and federal levels have diminished, at least temporarily, as a result of the economic downturn. The national economic situation has also caused the movement to restrict or control the shape of growth to ebb.

The "limit growth" philosophy is the result of two movements. The environmental movement is aimed at preserving scenic areas, the quality of our water and air, and wildlife. The second movement, whose constituency is concentrated among residents of rapidly growing communities, believes that new families force higher taxes, crowd local facilities, and adversely change the social climate.

It is not possible, at this time, to assess the long-term effects of current economic conditions or their impact on future public attitudes toward land use constraints by local, state, or federal agencies. There is some evidence, based on the offshore drilling controversy, that public resistance to at least some forms of growth has not diminished.

The objectives of this report are, first, to note the impact of broad changes in the location and composition of our population as these shifts may affect housing needs and, second, to assess the impact of traditional land use constraints on the type, location, and size of new housing, as well as the effects of more recent impact evaluation and fee requirements on the cost of housing.

A number of methods to encourage an increase in the supply of low- and moderate-income housing will be directly and indirectly discussed; housing issues that may be relevant to particular areas or communities will be briefly noted; and potential areas for effective action by responsible groups concerned with housing less affluent families will be listed.

It is useful to distinguish in these initial remarks between decent new housing for low-income households, which cannot be provided in the absence of some form of public subsidy, and moderate-income housing, whose supply can be expanded with innovative planning, improved construction techniques, and citizen involvement, which leads

---

*In 1972, mobile homes, which some exclude from the "decent housing" category, accounted for 30.5 percent of single-family private housing starts. Mobile homes, if properly constructed, can provide adequate housing, particularly in areas that lack public services.

to legislative action without requiring direct, large-scale government
funding.

EFFECTS OF POPULATION SHIFTS ON HOUSING

To provide a perspective on future land use/housing issues, it
is helpful to briefly note the effects of large-scale out-migration from
older states and regions—particularly from the Northeastern and
North Central states—to other areas of the nation. The continuing
net out-migration from nearly all large, high-density metropolitan
areas to exurban locations and smaller Standard Metropolitan Statistical Areas (SMSAs) will also influence the demand and availability of
low- and moderate-income housing in urban centers.

The current out-migration from aging urban areas should release substantial numbers of older units that, if properly maintained,
can be occupied by low- and moderate-income households. Many of
these households are concentrated in aging cities with continuing out-
migration, such as Detroit, Cleveland, and St. Louis. New York City,
for example, had a net out-migration of 300,000 persons between 1970
and 1973. The movement from large cities is not limited to white
families, either. Suburban Prince George's County, Maryland, has
increased its black population by 57 percent since 1970, reflecting the
out-migration of middle-income minorities from Washington, D.C.

In these older areas, it is not the availability of housing but
rather the ability to maintain such housing in the presence of unemployment, ghetto conditions, crime, and high local and state taxes
that burdens moderate-income households and that will be the critical
issue. In growing areas, adequate housing is a more urgent problem,
due to construction lags, but employment opportunities are greater
and tax burdens lower, allowing the "filtering" process to operate.

The annual national population increase has stabilized at about
0.7 percent in recent years. Since both white and black birthrates
are declining, the average household size is being reduced. However,
the number of children in minority households continues to be substantially higher than that of white families; as a result, these households
will require more housing space. On the average, however, low-
and moderate-income households will need smaller housing units to
satisfy "decent housing" criteria than is now the case. Such units are
concentrated in cities and inner suburbs, many of them having been
built prior to the movement of middle-income families to detached
housing in outer suburbs. Rehabilitation of these older units is therefore one means to expand the supply of such housing.

The pressure to build large, four- and five-bedroom land-inten-
sive housing on the periphery of urban areas should diminish as a re-

sult of demographics shifts, higher land costs, and other structural changes in the national economy.

The construction of smaller units in the future means a lower unit cost, which would allow a greater number of moderate-income households to obtain adequate new housing.

This somewhat optimistic view of future housing assumes a construction rate of close to 2 million units annually. Since new household formations resulting from the baby boom of the 1950s will soon reach their peak, the continuing depressed rate of housing starts will be particularly harmful to less affluent families, which are unable to compete for the existing housing stock.

LAND USE CONSTRAINTS

Types of Constraints

Housing is constrained to some degree in most urban communities by the imposition of various regulations, such as minimum house size and minimum lot requirements and specifications for building materials.

For example, an ordinance in Glassboro, New Jersey, requires, among other things, that 8 square feet of swimming pool or tennis court be provided for every 100 square feet of multiunit living space.* The aim of this ordinance was to limit new apartments to the "luxury" category. In many New Jersey communities and elsewhere, apartments are precluded by zoning. This in effect limits the number of moderate-income households in a jurisdiction, since the average income of apartment renters is substantially below that of owner-occupied housing residents. A typical ordinance, where zoning is available, restricts the number of bedrooms per apartment, effectively excluding large households.

Minimum lot size, or "exclusionary" zoning for detached housing units, is prevalent in many areas. Minimum lot sizes, which may vary from one to five acres, have been the subject of numerous legal challenges.

Obsolete building codes that contribute little to the quality of housing but increase housing costs are another implicit constraint. In addition, many communities require that the developer provide the infrastructure—roads, water, and sewer lines—that may have previously been the direct fiscal responsibility of local government.

---

*For examples of various constraints, see Norman Williams and Thomas Norman, "Exclusionary Land Use Controls," Land Use Controls Quarterly (Fall 1970).

The imposition of fees and other charges that require direct or indirect payments by developers for public facilities as a part of the rezoning or the building permit process is among measures being adopted by many communities. In these jurisdictions, developers, in addition to deeding land, have to provide funds for schools, parks, and other facilities that will be used by future occupants of new housing units. This frequently requires an initial cash layout by the developer, who anticipates recovering the outlay from future purchasers and renters. This ultimately shifts most of the cost to the future resident and thereby increases the purchase price.

A somewhat different cost arises from having to submit state or locally mandated environmental and other impact statements. Both California and Florida legislation require such reports when new private construction is initiated. Frequently original plans have to be revised and facilities expanded by the developer to obtain building approval. For example, in one Florida community a developer is being asked to build and equip a fire station as a precondition to initiating a large-scale housing project. These requirements frequently delay construction, increasing the cost to the builder and ultimately, given our inflationary economy, to the consumer. Various sewer moratoriums also limit land areas where new housing can locate and probably increase the cost of land and thus the price of dwellings.

Rationale for Regulations and Fees

It would be erroneous to conclude that most land use constraints are directly aimed at keeping "undesirable" families and minorities from residing in a community. Constraints are generally directed at achieving specific economic, social, and environmental objectives.

In many cases, constraints are imposed in an attempt to assure that the type of housing constructed is similar or better than the existing housing stock in value and appearance in order to "protect" the property owners, whose political strength—as a result of greater participation in local issues, higher probability of voting, and support of candidates—exceeds that of renters.

Many of the constraints reduce the likelihood of implicit fiscal subsidies from existing residents to new households that result when the amount to be spent on public services exceeds the revenues obtained from families moving in. The broader issue raised by these economic factors is whether a community has a legal or moral right to limit new households to essentially those who can pay their way.

The major concern of middle- and upper-income neighborhoods in regard to new residents is, however, probably more social than economic. It has been shown from surveys that, while local officials

recognize that most apartments produce a fiscal surplus, they frequently oppose renters because they are perceived as being transient,
more prone to violence, and having social values that differ from those
of owner-occupied families.

From the perspective of the property owner, the various land
use constraints that limit the supply of housing in his community are
economically beneficial, since the higher prices that may result from
limiting construction increases the value of his property. The community property tax base is also expanded without a parallel increase
in the demand for public services. It is the prospective resident and
the present renter who are placed at a disadvantage. The environmental statements are aimed at ensuring that the quality of the air, water,
and soil is maintained in the community. Improving the environment,
it is argued, benefits the entire public, particularly low- and moderate-income households, which do not have the mobility of the more
affluent and thus suffer most from degradation of the environment in
their community.

Impact of Land Use Constraints and Fees
on Moderate-Income Housing

Individually, the various direct and implicit constraints have
little impact on the total quantity of moderate-income housing produced, but they significantly influence the location of housing, particularly new housing aimed at those with average incomes. Collective-
ly, land use and construction requirements, fees, and impact statements do increase the selling price of all housing units, regardless of
location. It is important to understand, however, that these additional
outlays, many of which indeed improve the quality of housing and the
surrounding environment, account for only a small percentage of the
rise in housing costs in recent years. Increased construction worker
wages, the higher cost of building material, and higher land prices
explain the dominant share of rising costs. Most of these factors are
directly linked to labor contracts and the national economy and are
thus essentially beyond the direct control of local government and
concerned citizens.

There is little empirical data showing the effects of various
fees, requirements for impact evaluation, and related regulations
on the selling prices of houses or on rents. Since regulations and
their enforcement differ even among communities in the same region,
generalizations are not possible. As a rough estimate, they may add
from 2 to 5 percent to the purchase price of a typical unit, depending
on the time it takes to process an application. When this additional
outlay is combined with the inefficiencies that result from traditional

zoning and related controls, costs may increase by 10 or perhaps 15 percent.

It should be obvious that, even if all existing land use constraints, regardless of their merits, were to be removed, the number of moderate-income housing units constructed would not increase substantially, while the number of new low-income units would be completely unaffected. Reducing the selling price of a unit from $40,000 to $36,000 or even $32,000 is hardly likely to result in a housing boom in the $12,000 to $15,000 price range. Reducing the cost by 10 percent or so would help to the degree that investment may be shifted from other areas into housing. It would also help households whose income is currently close to the threshold of being able to purchase or rent satisfactory housing.

ACTIVITIES TO STIMULATE HOUSING

Although the greatest focus of housing activists has been on challenging the legality of land use constraints, there is little evidence that even their total elimination would significantly affect the level of moderate-income housing units constructed. Therefore, the encouragement of additional construction—both middle-income and moderate-income housing—by incentives or regulation appears to be a more useful approach to alleviating shortages that may exist.

Encouraging the Construction of Middle-Income Housing

As already noted, only a small share of new housing is aimed at low- and moderate-income families. However, expanding the supply of housing directed at middle-income families indirectly increases housing opportunities for lower-income households (those having incomes of less than $3,000 in 1965 dollars). Moderate-income families, however, benefit the most from the chain of moves initiated when a middle-income housing unit is occupied.* New developments in the suburbs have contributed to improved housing conditions for less affluent families by vacating older housing within central cities during the last two decades.

The major limitation of encouraging middle-income housing construction in suburbs is that it results in greater economic and fis-

---

*For a discussion of these effects, see John B. Lansing et al., New Homes and Poor People (Ann Arbor: Survey Research Center, University of Michigan, 1969).

cal disparities between the core and outer areas, which can lead to
various forms of segregation. The major advantage of this approach
is that housing opportunities for all groups can be expanded while the
need to provide large subsidies to moderate-income families is reduced. Providing housing allowances to enable these families to have
their choice of housing encourages the "filtering" process.

Encouraging Construction of Moderate-Income Units

Moderate-income housing can be encouraged for specific types
of large-scale development—particularly planned unit developments
(PUDs) and new communities—by the acceptance of "fair share" housing at the regional level and by requiring such housing as part of nonresidential land use change approval.

Planned Unit Developments

Large PUDs now form a substantial share of new housing, particularly in Florida. This large-scale constuction rarely includes provisions for low- or even moderate-income housing at present. The
benefits that derive to the developer as a result of a PUD that has been
approved by the local government provide an opportunity to negotiate
for the construction of a specified number of lower priced units with
the incentive density bonuses or other benefits that will increase the
profitability of higher priced units. Such negotiations are most likely
to be successful if a large area, such as a multicounty region, im-
plements these policies. This has been the case in the Developments
of Regional Impact (DRI) review process undertaken by the South
Eastern Florida Planning Council, which includes five counties.

A less desirable alternative would be to impose a requirement
that a certain percentage of the units be provided for large residential
developments, such as those that include 500 or more units. Such
requirements are subject to legal challenges and may prove to be
counterproductive in the long run.

Industrial and Commercial Development

Most communities are anxious to attract nonresidential, particularly industrial, development to improve their fiscal position and aid
local business firms. They are less anxious, or even unwilling, to
modify their land use controls to permit new housing designed to meet
the needs of moderate-income employees attracted by a new facility,
a situation that can result in long journeys to work. It also provides
fiscal benefits to one community, while the cost of providing services

to moderate-income families is shifted to nearby jurisdictions that
have housing that the new workers can afford.

A requirement that new housing (if sufficient vacancies are un-
available) be provided for a specified share of the labor force within a
certain radius of large nonresidential facilities could provide more
housing opportunities to moderate-income households and indirectly
aid communities that cannot attract new industry.

New Communities

A major factor in the federal government's decision to back
"new towns" was the belief that totally planned communities would,
from an economic perspective, be better able to build, and their residents more willing to accommodate, low- and moderate-income housing. However, the new community diversified housing concept has
virtually faded away, in part because the federal government has made
few grants or subsidies for low- and moderate-income residents. As
some of the developers of these new communities have stated, the
absence of federal aid will make these new towns just another middle-
class suburb, which is essentially what Reston, Virginia (not part of
the new town program backed by HUD) has become.

It has become increasingly obvious that low-, and frequently
moderate-, income housing cannot be provided without direct government aid even in a new town, where housing is no less (and in some
cases more) expensive to construct than in other places. The alternative—to mandate such housing—does not appear economically feasible given the financial pressures on most new towns, which are strug-
gling for survival. New communities, it is evident, will not be the
means to even marginally expand housing opportunities for the less
affluent in the foreseeable future.

"Fair Share" Housing

"Fair share" housing plans are aimed at distributing low- and
moderate-income housing requirements among a group of communities
—frequently suburbs of central cities—taking into account the economic
status of a jurisdiction, the level of the existing moderate-income housing stock, and environmental and other factors.

The major advantage of such agreements is that each community,
as well as its neighbors, takes in a "fair share," which makes the
process more acceptable politically and sounder from the economic and
social perspectives. The major tool for requiring implementation
by a region has been the A-95 review process, which can withhold federal sewer and water treatment facilities to local jurisdictions.

Up to now, most fair share plans have not been successful, for three reasons: the absence of federal subsidies, strong political resistance, and reversals of low- and moderate-income housing requirements by the courts, as in the case of Fairfax County, Virginia, which adopted an ordinance to construct a certain percentage of housing aimed at less affluent families.

Despite initial failures and slow progress, such plans have significant advantages over concentrated, high-density public housing in central cities, which imposes great social costs on a region. However, more public relations work and more innovative planning will be required even after federal housing subsidy funds become available to win acceptance of this approach by local residents.

OTHER LAND USE/HOUSING ISSUES

In addition to the major issues already discussed, a number of other areas require attention by those concerned about improving housing opportunities.

Rural Housing

While urban housing is the main focus of those concerned with housing problems, rural needs should not be ignored. One must recognize, however, that their problems are not similar. Unlike in urban areas, overcrowding is not an issue, and rural households only allocate a small percentage of their income—about 10 to 12 percent—for housing, in part because of lower construction costs and taxes. Structural deficiencies—primarily plumbing—which relate to inadequate water and sewage treatment facilities, are common. About 19 percent of rural homes do not have full plumbing.

Land use issues in rural areas are primarily concerned with the lack of any zoning or health and general land use related environmental standards. It is not too much control but rather too little local monitoring that is perhaps the major problem.

Some proposals have been offered, including an administration plan for Direct Cash Assistance (DCA) to rural households. It has been estimated that 1.5 million rural households live in substandard housing. Among the groups most affected are the elderly (over half of all substandard housing units are occupied by older households), migrant workers, and American Indians. Increasing employment opportunities in rural areas is the most efficient means of improving housing for those who are able to work. Direct subsidies—particularly those for the elderly aimed at improving structural deficiencies—

could improve the status of rural housing for others who are unable to work.

In-Migration of Middle-Income Households to Central Cities

In some cities there appears to be a reverse in-migration of young, affluent households to neighborhoods where the older housing stock is being rehabilitated. From a general economic and social perspective, such movement is beneficial to the city. In addition, it can reduce some of the land conversion pressure in the outer suburbs. However, in the absence of controls, one adverse effect may be a reduced stock of moderate-income housing. The conversion of older apartments to condominiums aimed at middle-income households can create a similar reduction in moderately priced housing.

Since net out-migration from many large cities is continuing, it is difficult to determine the extent of this problem.

High-Density Housing

It has been argued by some that constructing high-density housing is a more efficient means of providing living quarters from both a public and a private cost perspective. In fact, high-density cities have substantially higher per capita costs for almost all services compared to lower-density suburban communities and moderate-size (50,000 to 100,000 residents) cities. The cost of construction, on a square-foot basis, is also higher. Thus, such housing provides no economic advantage, even if social problems, such as higher crime, could be overcome.

Pressures on Small Developers

Various land use regulations, impact statements, and other controls, in combination with economic pressures, have a tendency to place the small developer at a disadvantage. The trend for large corporate involvement in land use and housing has, in a number of cases, been reversed. However, the long-run pattern appears to be for large organizations to control much of the housing market.

This pattern could well be to the disadvantage of the housing industry. Moderate-income housing requirements may become more difficult to impose if large corporations dominate the industry. There is no evidence of lower housing costs resulting from large-scale labor-

HUNT LIBRARY
CARNEGIE-MELLON UNIVERSITY
PITTSBURGH, PENNSYLVANIA 15213

intensive building activity. Therefore, few benefits can result from
reducing the number of small developers in the housing industry.

CONCLUSION

While local land use constraints have been cited by some, including segments of the housing industry, as a major factor in the low
volume of new, unsubsidized moderate-income units, there is little
evidence that this is actually the case. In the early 1960s, when land
use was not an issue, few new detached housing units were constructed
in suburbs for the moderate-income family market. Eliminating
many of the constraints would not substantially increase the volume
of construction in the absence of federal government programs designed to promote such housing, although the location of some new
housing would change.

Most state-mandated land use legislation has a neutral effect
on moderate-income housing, although the legislation usually acknowl-
edges housing needs for all residents. It is unlikely, given the present
political climate, that state or regional agencies will use land use
legislation as a lever to force the construction of more units for
lower-income families. Therefore, Congress and local governments
remain the arenas for encouraging such housing, directly or indirectly
by land use legislation. As noted previously, general economic expansion and increased levels of middle-income housing construction
can contribute to, but cannot fully meet, the housing needs of low-income families, particularly those residing in central cities.

The use of coercive measures to expand low- and moderate-
income housing could well be counterproductive, leading to further
out-migration of middle-income households and jobs from urban
areas, where the need is greatest. Noncoercive legislation, which
uses the local government's land use power to the benefit of both the
developer and the residents, appears to be one means of encouraging
such housing.

In addition to this general problem, a number of other issues,
which have been briefly noted, require public awareness. These include rural housing needs, efforts by some to encourage moderate-
income housing at high densities, and pressures on small developers.

The overall conclusion is that land use legislation is an important, but not critical, issue. The major negative aspect of land use
legislation is that it shifts the location of moderate-income housing
rather than severely constraining its production. This, in turn,
leads to a concentration of lower-income households in some neighborhoods and communities, which can create both economic and social
problems.

2

THE NEED FOR NEW
HOUSING FINANCING
TECHNIQUES

The two most significant factors in housing during the past decade have been the rapid rise in price of houses and the even more rapid rise in the required monthly or annual payments per dollar of purchase price. As a result of these two pressures, the payments needed to live in a new house today are about 240 percent of what they were only 10 years ago. The average housing expense for a new house is probably 350 percent of what it was 20 years ago.

This is a clear reflection of the impact of inflation on the problem of providing decent housing for every American family, which has been our expressed goal for 25 years. While inflation has raised the incomes of some families, increases have lagged far behind needed housing payments. The rate of growth in average household income during the past decade has probably been only half the growth in required housing payments. The gap for the housing needy has been even greater. Those most in need of housing aid are the elderly and those families without someone in the employed labor force. These groups have fallen even further behind under the pressure of inflation. Their incomes have not kept pace with the soaring costs of food, fuel, and housing.

We still lack a full understanding of what inflation does to normal economic relationships. Furthermore, many of our government leaders and those who shape public opinion take the attitude that we should not consider plans for mitigating the bad effects of inflation, because if we succeed in reducing the suffering that accompanies it, the pressure to fight it will be lessened. The possibility that we will not try hard enough concerns me, too; but the unnecessary hardships suffered by many concern me more.

This chapter will first outline some of the ways in which inflation creates problems for housing and then examine some of the cur-

rent government housing financing programs and show how they can
assist the housing needy.

INTEREST RATES AND INFLATION

In the early 1950s, the market yield on FHA mortgages was under 4.25 percent. During 1974, the rate rose to over 10.25 percent.
Since interest—even in the middle of this range—accounts for one-half
or more of total housing expenses, it is obviously a major factor in
the rise of total housing expenditures. What is the relationship between this increase in interest payments and inflation?

To understand how inflation affects housing, we must recognize
the difference between real interest rates and nominal interest rates.
Nominal interest rates are simply contract rates in current dollars,
with no correction made for any changes that may occur in the purchasing power of the dollar. Real interest rates are nominal rates that
have been corrected to take into account any change in the purchasing
power (value) of the dollar during the period a loan is outstanding.

By subtracting the expected rate of inflation from the contract
(nominal) interest rate, we find the real interest rate. For example,
most observers believe that lenders would be very happy to receive a
real rate of return of 4 percent on a loan of money for one year. They
would expect to lend $100 and get back $104. But if prices rise 6 percent during that year, the $104 the lender gets back will buy fewer
goods than the $100 he lent initially. The lender thus receives no real
interest.

People with capital who expect prices to rise try to avoid such
a loss in purchasing power. One way to do so is to invest directly in
goods, commodities, or real property. If they hold assets whose
prices rise with inflation, they will be better off than if they had lent
dollars that will be worth less in purchasing power when they are re-
turned.

A would-be borrower of money during an inflation will have to
promise an interest rate high enough to offset part of the loss in the
purchasing power of the money he will pay back. Some of the high
interest rates currently being paid are designed to insure that the
real interest rate is high enough to make it worthwhile for the lenders
to lend.

Since everyone has a different view of how great inflation may
be and many people lack the ability to protect themselves, there are
no exact estimates, but it appears that a major reason for the higher
interest rates we are now paying is the high rate of inflation we have
been experiencing in recent years. These rates also reflect greater
uncertainties and risks with respect to what money will be worth.

Inflationary Interest Rates and Mortgage Lending

Inflationary interest rates aggravate the problems of housing in three ways: they raise current payments above current incomes, they add to uncertainties, and they distort flows of money through lending institutions.

Mortgage Payments Versus Income

Let us examine first the problem of mortgage payments and income. Assume that a buyer can find a house for sale at $25,000. To meet the standard payments at a 4 percent interest rate, the buyer would—according to recent relationships—be expected to have a monthly income of $950, although some buyers with net assets rather than other debts might have a monthly income as low as $700. With a 6 percent inflation rate, however, and a resultant 10 percent interest rate, the buyer would have to have an average monthly income of about $1,700. (Again, in special cases, a buyer with an income of $1,250 a month might qualify.)

The lesson is clear. Inflation causes debt service to nearly double. The number of families that can qualify to meet the payments for a $25,000 house is cut by probably one-half to two-thirds.

Moreover, a type of "Catch-22" situation exists. If a 6 percent rate of inflation raises contract interest rates to 10 percent, prospective buyers find that they would be well-off if they could buy a house; but the required payments are so high that they cannot afford to do so. The catch is that at the same time that inflation forces up interest rates, it also raises the value, and consequently the owners' equities, in their houses. (Equity equals the difference between the value of the house and the amount owed on it.) Most of the high interest rates are reflected in a concurrent buildup in equity and added saving, but families cannot buy houses under these conditions.

For instance, compare the situation of a family buying a $25,000 house with a 30-year mortgage of $23,500 in a period with no inflation, 4 percent mortgages, and little or no change in housing prices with the situation of a family purchasing the same house in a period with 6 percent inflation, 10 percent interest rates, and the price of the house rising at 6 percent a year. We have already noted that, in inflation, debt service payments will almost double. But most of the difference in debt payments will be accompanied by an annual 6 percent increase in the value of the house and in the owner's equity. If the owner were to sell the house at the end of 10 years of inflation, he would expect to receive $40,000-45,000 for it, or $20,000-25,000 cash after paying off the rest of the mortgage. In contrast, with no inflation and a 4 percent mortgage, he would sell it for something less than $25,000 and would realize only a small amount of cash after paying off the mortgage.

Unfortunately, families do not have the choice of making the larger payments. At 10 percent interest rates, the typical mortgage contract calls for saving so much through debt service payments that most families do not have enough income left over even for normal expenses. The 10 percent interest rate, accompanied by rising housing prices, is equivalent to saving $2,000-3,000 a year; but families cannot afford to make the necessary payments. Instead, they are unable to buy a house. They end up with poorer housing and less, not more, savings. They could afford the house with the lower, but not with the higher, debt payments.

The answer to this problem is some form of graduated payment mortgage, perhaps with a flexible maturity and a variable interest rate.

If interest rates are 10 percent, because of inflation, a logical mortgage might call for monthly payments below the interest rate, with the difference being added to the debt. The family would pay only two-thirds or so of the debt service normally required at a 10 percent interest rate. The assumption is that, if the house were sold, its increased value would pay off the large remaining mortgage, which might actually be greater than it was when the house was bought.

The debt could also be paid off if family income were to rise as a result of inflation. Or, if inflation slowed down, a variable mortgage rate would allow the interest charge to fall so that more payments could be made on the debt.

To those of us accustomed to thinking about mortgage payments and interest rates under noninflationary conditions, these proposed solutions seem preposterous. They are not. They are a realistic and sensible response to the problem of inflation. In an inflation, financial relationships become upended. Unless we try to understand them and plan ways of meeting their distortions, we will end up with a chronic shortage of housing.

Increased Risks and Uncertainties

In addition to being hard to understand, graduated payment mortgages are unpopular because they seem to increase risks and uncertainties. We think of the debt repayment on the mortgage as a safety factor for the lender. If the family loses its source of income or breaks up, the greater equity is a protection for the lender. Of course, inflation offers the lender the same protection. If the equity has gone up, the source of the income has little effect on the risks.

Savings Institutions

Recently—as in many times in the past—even those who might
be able to afford high interest rates are finding little or no mortgage
money available. The reason for this is that rapidly shifting interest
rates put great pressure on savings institutions. Their assets are
tied up at fixed rates. They have trouble paying current inflationary
market interest rates. Knowledgeable savers—who are also the
largest savers—withdraw their money and put it into government bonds
or other assets that pay higher rates. Mortgage money disappears.
Ceilings on interest rates cannot solve the problem. Savers
have the choices of buying property, commodities, stocks, land, gold,
or anything else that promises to keep their purchasing power protected against inflation. If lenders are not allowed to receive a positive real interest rate, no money will be available to borrow. Where
usury laws have set negative real interest rates, there has been no
money for housing.
One solution is to shift the assets of saving institutions to more
flexible mortgages with variable interest rates so that they can pay
more flexible rates to their depositors. If savers can be protected
against negative real interest rates, the flow of funds to both deposit
institutions and the housing industry can be made more stable.
Another possibility would be to allow savings institutions to offer
deposits with a purchasing-power correction or guarantee against inflation to small savers. Such accounts would guarantee a small real
rate of interest. The rate at which depositors would be credited
would vary with the degree of inflation. Because few institutions can
afford to take the risks of violent inflation, the government would
have to assume the risks of price changes of more than 5 percent.
The actual mechanics of such guarantees are relatively simple. With
negligible cost or disruption to existing institutions, the typical
small saver can be insured so that he will not lose when he holds such
a guaranteed savings account. These guarantees would also ensure a
much steadier flow of mortgage funds to the housing market.

SOURCES OF FINANCING

We are now in a period of turmoil with respect to how public
support will be granted for housing. The Housing and Community
Development Act of 1974 completely revamped many of the federal
programs. At the same time, an increasing number of state housing
finance agencies have sprung up. HUD is in the process of issuing

regulations under the new act. Their final form will depend not only on development, but also on the reaction of groups such as ICH.

It is difficult at this time to describe these programs in detail, since they are in flux. I shall therefore simply point them out and discuss some of the problems and opportunities they offer. A principal function of a group such as ICH is to be a pressure group to try to ensure decent housing for low- and moderate-income groups. Unless they are carefully monitored, housing policies have a tendency to aid those other than the needy.

Another major function ICH can perform is to become an innovator and a creative manipulator of the public regulations. Who gets what in the housing programs depends less on the laws than on how they are interpreted and operated.

ICH can also be a vital force in assuring that the consumer interest is represented. Most housing programs are oriented toward lenders or producers. Both groups have full-time interests in the programs and the time and the money to protect these interests. The failure of consumers to be adequately represented in the production process is to their disadvantage.

Finally, although ICH has a stake as a nonprofit developer of housing, it should recognize that this stake is tenuous. Conventional wisdom holds that management of nonprofit groups has been so poor as to negate other advantages they may have. As a result, public policy now seems to be one of cutting back the role of nonprofit developers. Offsetting this policy will require better management and proof that the special functions ICH can perform cannot be handled elsewhere.

The following seven aspects of the current situation in regard to public support of housing will be briefly discussed:

1. Section 8 housing
2. Community development block grants
3. Farmers Home Administration
4. State housing finance agencies
5. Income tax benefits
6. Mobile homes
7. Special problems of the elderly

Section 8 Housing

The major subsidized programs under the new Housing and Community Development Act are to be handled through Section 8. The critical factor is that HUD has the authority to contract for assistance payments with nonprofit or similar organizations as well as with for-profit corporations if it deems this to be a proper procedure. The contracts are to be awarded on the basis of proposals from interested developers or rehabilitators. HUD is to choose those proposals it considers most likely to meet the program's goals.

Under Section 8, the subsidies to individual households can be more flexible than under previous laws. A section of the grants is to be reserved for projects for the elderly. FHA mortgage guarantees are available under Sections 221, 231, and 213. Mortgages can apparently be 100 percent to nonprofit groups. In addition, HUD is authorized to reestablish a direct-loan program for the elderly under the 202 program, but interest rates will be only slightly below the market rate.

Key problems will arise regarding the role of nonprofit developers, the availability of final financing, and construction loans. In most cases, HUD has a good deal of flexibility in the basic law and in GNMA authority. How HUD will use the authority remains to be seen. Unless good procedures are developed, many serious problems will remain.

I would like to see nonprofit sponsorship of cooperative apartments under housing assistance contracts. Such programs have the advantage of greater individual flexibility while using the family's desire to be a homeowner to increase efficiency.

Community Development Block Grants

The general redevelopment programs and model city programs have been replaced with new block grants with far more authority being given to the locality as to how the money will be used. Many communities will be added to these programs for the first time.

It is in this sphere that some of the most creative programs are possible. They must be tied to the general purpose of redevelopment and rehabilitation, but housing for low- and moderate-income groups might be stimulated by lease of land for housing at low or nominal rates. Payments might be made for supportive services in relocation, staff training, and organization of housing projects. Revolving funds can be set up to make construction possible.

Farmers Home Administration

One of the active housing programs that is frequently neglected is that of the Farmers Home Administration (FmHA). This agency makes below-market direct housing loans in rural areas. It is the type of program whose use can increase rapidly if groups such as ICH call to the attention of their members their availability. Aid in preparing loan applications can also be extremely helpful.

State Housing Finance Agencies

A majority of the states have housing finance agencies. Their powers vary. Most of them issue tax-exempt bonds to aid in mortgage lending. They also make use of the majority of federal programs and could play a major role in Section 8 housing. They are sources of junior mortgages; tax abatement; and, in some cases, mortgage insurance. In some states they acquire land and may develop it.

An examination of state programs has considerable value, because the state governments have been more flexible than the federal government. They have, for example, recognized the problem of inflation and interest rates and have experimented with flexible and graduated payments. They have also been sources of the type of development and management aid required by many nonprofit sponsors. IC H-affiliate agencies are a logical source of ideas, clients, and sponsorship for the state agencies.

Income Tax Benefits

When we search for the largest subsidies in the housing field, we find that they come through the tax benefits—such as accelerated depreciation—granted to private developers. How many have attempted to use this subsidy source? It would seem logical for agencies to plan projects and design buildings and then lease them from private builders. Because the builders can retain the tax benefits, the rentals under the leases should be at far lower rates than if they were to own the buildings themselves.

Granting that tax laws are complex, it is still probably worth examining the possible use of charitable gifts. There are many situations in which the gift of a building to a church group could be made with only a slight cost to the donor, with the possibility always present that he might actually increase his profits through the gift.

Most of us hesitate to take full advantage of the subsidy programs established by Congress, but we ought to face this type of question squarely. When Congress establishes tax policies to aid housing, should the subsidies be rejected?

Mobile Homes

Recent studies have shown that mobile homes form a major sector for which consumer representation is needed. There are excellent mobile home parks, occupied primarily by the elderly, in resort areas. The various public programs such as Section 8 and FHA provide for the use of mobile homes. Such programs make a great deal of sense when capital is expensive. The amount of capital tied up in a mobile unit is far less than in a large house. It follows that the higher the interest rates, the greater the value of mobile homes in comparison to traditional housing. With mobile homes many of the delays in planning and construction can be avoided. A price estimated in advance is likely to be far firmer, and the risk of cost overruns is much smaller. These projects can be operated as cooperatives or as rental housing.

Special Problems of the Elderly

The problem of inflation is particularly acute for the elderly, because most of them live on limited fixed incomes. That is why a solution to their housing problems is so difficult. They cannot afford to pay the inflationary nominal interest rates, because their income does not rise with prices.

There are several ways to attack this problem. If an elderly person owns a house, it may be possible to buy his equity with an annuity guaranteeing him a place to live to the end of his life. An inflation that causes values to rise would then improve, not endanger, his housing. In the same way, it may be possible to periodically recalculate values using a type of graduated payment in which the largest share is paid upon death or the move to a nursing home.

CONCLUSION

The standard approach to housing has always been to assume that inflation is a temporary phenomenon. While we may hope this is true, we cannot afford to stop building while we wait to see what the outcome of the battle will be. The cost in current distress through poor housing is too great.

Instead, we must reexamine all of our financing devices to see if we can remove the uncertainties and risks that inflation introduces. One approach is to improve flexibility in payments between borrowers and lenders so that the need for the high-risk premiums required by unyielding contracts can be removed. Another approach is to have the government assume more of the risks of inflation. The government is one of the few economic entities that profits from inflation. Some of these profits should be pledged to better uses.

If the government has to assume more responsibility for the costs of inflation, it will probably devote more time to seeing that its policies make sense. This is far from the case in the housing field at present. ICH can help improve our policies by gaining a better understanding of them and learning how to utilize them to the fullest possible extent by acting as a pressure group for their improvement.

3

NEIGHBORHOOD
PRESERVATION

The 1949 Housing Act established the goal of a "decent home and a suitable living environment for every American family." Twenty-five years of federal, state, and local housing programs have not achieved this goal; for sure, progress has been made from the dark days of tenement housing squalor, but acres of deteriorating and abandoned buildings in every urban area attest to the bankruptcy of the nation's housing programs. This chapter will first present an overview of past housing philosophies and then focus on neighborhood preservation—an emerging program now advocated as an idea whose time has come.

URBAN RENEWAL: THE 1950s' FEDERAL BULLDOZER

Urban renewal was the post–World War II approach to satisfying the goal set forth in the 1949 Housing Act. Slums would be demolished and new housing and commercial facilities constructed; decaying core neighborhoods would be replaced by thriving commercial and residential areas.

Urban renewal must be credited with eliminating some of the nation's worst slums. It was also responsible for the economic renaissance of some downtown business areas. As a housing strategy, however, urban renewal was largely a failure. Considerably more units were destroyed than were built. Moreover, the replacement housing was often far too expensive for the residents whose housing had been destroyed by the federal urban renewal bulldozer.

By the end of the 1950s, the philosophy and application of urban renewal was in disrepute, and a new housing strategy was called for. This proved to be housing rehabilitation.

HOUSING REHABILITATION: THE STRATEGY
OF THE 1960s

The urban renewal thesis provoked the rehabilitation antithesis.
President Kennedy, in his 1961 housing message, stated:

> As we broaden the scope of the renewal program
> looking toward newer and brighter urban areas
> we must move with new vigor to conserve and re-
> habilitate existing residential districts. Our in-
> vestment in non-farm residential real estate is es-
> timated at about 500 billion dollars—the largest
> single component in our national wealth. These
> assets must be used responsibly, consumed and
> supplemented and not neglected or wasted in our
> emphasis on the new.

Presidents Johnson and Nixon expressed similar support for
rehabilitation. During their administrations, Congress enacted scores
of financing programs to encourage renovation as well as new construction, such as the Section 221(d)(3) and 236 subsidies, which financed multifamily rehabilitation, and the Section 235 program, which
aided the renovation of single-family homes.
The rehabilitation track record was largely mixed. Touted as
a high-volume, low-cost, socially sensitive strategy, rehabilitation
did provide many housing units, but neither as cheaply nor as easily
as had been expected. Even more cause for alarm were the numerous
rehabilitation projects that experienced initial success but soon suc-
cumbed to inner city social and neighborhood pathologies. This de-
nouement led the federal government to put a moratorium on all rehabilitation and new construction subsidies. Neighborhood preservation has emerged as the postmoratorium housing strategy and is likely
to become the housing philosophy and strategy of the 1970s.

NEIGHBORHOOD PRESERVATION: THE STRATEGY
OF THE 1970s

There is currently widespread support for, and interest in,
neighborhood preservation. The Institute of Real Estate Management
(IREM) has described this strategy as an "idea whose time has come."
The December 1974 issue of Architectural Record focused on the advantages of neighborhood conservation. It hailed conservation as a
"positive tool for preserving the essential character and human values
of cities and towns." It concluded that "the surge of interest and at-

tention to the re-use of older buildings—call it rehab or remodelling
or recycling or modernization—amounts to nothing less than a revolu-
tion in attitude"—and a welcome change at that.

The October 1974 publication of the National Association of
Housing and Redevelopment Officials, Journal of Housing, discussed
neighborhood preservation, focusing on conservation efforts in Washington, D.C. The general need for preservation was analyzed and the
specifics of the Washington case study were examined.

A growing number of conferences, papers, and studies have
treated and will treat the neighborhood preservation strategy. A
Charleston, South Carolina, conference conducted in February 1975
stated as its theme "neighborhood preservation and rehabilitation."
The National Association of Housing and Redevelopment Officials held
a conference in May 1975 on "urban homesteading and neighborhood
conservation." In February 1975 the Real Estate Research Corporation and the Rutgers University Center for Urban Policy Research
completed a study for HUD surveying innovative local neighborhood
preservation programs. In 1971 the Urban Collaborative submitted
an analysis to the Michigan State Housing Development Authority de-
tailing a neighborhood conservation program. This represents only
a partial listing of the outpouring of conferences and literature calling
for a neighborhood preservation strategy.

Last, but not least, is growing federal, state, and local support
for neighborhood conservation. The 1974 Housing and Community Development Act explicitly supports the neighborhood preservation effort. As it states:

> The Congress further finds that policies designed to
> contribute to the achievement of the national housing
> goal have not directed sufficient attention and re-
> sources to the preservation of existing houses and
> neighborhoods, that the deterioration and abandon-
> ment of housing for the nation's lower income families
> has accelerated over the last decade, and that this
> acceleration has contributed to neighborhood disinte-
> gration and partially negated the program toward
> achieving the national housing goal which has been
> made primarily through new construction. . . .
>   The Congress declares that if the national
> housing goal is to be achieved, a greater effort
> must be made to encourage the preservation of
> existing housing and neighborhoods through such
> measures as housing preservation, moderate rehabili-
> tation and improvements in housing management
> and maintenance, in conjunction with the provision
> of adequate municipal services.

The federal government has not been alone in embracing the neighborhood conservation approach. Numerous states and localities have similarly shifted some of their housing focus away from new construction or isolated rehabilitation programs to the more comprehensive and flexible preservation route. New Jersey, for example, provided its urban localities with block grants in 1975 to enable them to establish local preservation efforts of their own. New York City and Washington, D.C., as well as other localities, are effecting or encouraging neighborhood preservation programs.

Preservation appears to be in its incipient stage and will soon become omnipresent. Demolition and new construction dominated housing policy in the 1950s, rehabilitation came to the fore in the 1960s, and preservation appears to be the heir apparent of the 1970s and beyond. But this shift merely begs the question of what neighborhood conservation is and why it is being espoused as a strategy.

WHAT IS NEIGHBORHOOD PRESERVATION?

Preservation is the strategy of physically and socially rebuilding or preserving a neighborhood fiber. It is an all-inclusive term that refers predominantly to the rehabilitation of housing but also includes demolition, re-use of space, some new construction, and a series of supportive socioeconomic strategies. One major aspect of the preservation approach involves the definition and selection of particular neighborhood environments and the matching of these neighborhoods to a set of public subsidy commitments designed to improve and maintain the social and physical infrastructure.

There are a number of premises to the neighborhood preservation program. Preservation has a commitment to recycling the extant housing stock and neighborhoods; it is opposed to the demolition/ new construction focus of early urban renewal. It does recognize, however, that selective demolition and new construction may be appropriate under certain neighborhood conditions.

Neighborhood preservation recognizes the variety and dynamic nature of urban neighborhoods and attempts to devise suitable supportive strategies for this broad range of conditions. It also views the neighborhood as a spatial/social rallying point around which urban communities can be stabilized or rejuvenated.

Neighborhood preservation is a comprehensive strategy. It encompasses a broad range of physical, social, and economic supportive efforts, including rehabilitation, employment training, and commercial funding. It also attempts to involve private input with the public contributions made by federal, state, and local governments.

Neighborhood preservation is also a flexible strategy. It is eclectic in approach, combining rehabilitation, redevelopment, and other strategies as deemed needed. This pragmatism contrasts with past housing strategies, which tended to have a one-dimensional nature, often consisting of only new construction or only rehabilitation. The neighborhood preservation approach also attempts to apply those strategies most applicable in different neighborhoods; it strives to tailor its remedies to fit the different ailments of various areas.

Neighborhood preservation maintains its supportive strategies on a long-term basis, though it may vary the magnitude and variety of its aids as neighborhood conditions improve or deteriorate. Preservation constitutes not a one-shot infusion of assistance but rather a sustained nurturing process. To improve the viability of this long-term application, explicit attention is given to monitoring and feedback on the interface between changing neighborhood conditions and applied/ needed supportive strategies.

WHY NEIGHBORHOOD PRESERVATION?

The advantages of neighborhood preservation can best be defined by comparing it with earlier housing strategies. Past housing efforts often emphasized demolition and new construction, while preservation is committed to recycling extant housing and neighborhoods—an essential approach given existing energy and environmental constraints. In this respect, neighborhood preservation is similar to housing rehabilitation but is far more comprehensive and responsive to a broad scale of local needs (see Figure 1).

Earlier programs were often applied without modification to all neighborhoods and without taking into consideration varying area environments. They also tended to be project oriented, without taking into consideration the outside forces that will affect the housing that is built or renovated. The Section 236 program, for example, had a strong project focus and tended to be applied in a similar fashion in both slums and stable neighborhoods and in urban and rural neighborhoods. Preservation, in contrast, is more concerned with the larger environment of the neighborhood than with just the project.

Past housing programs claimed to be comprehensive but rarely actually achieved this goal. In most cases they supported a narrow range of housing efforts—only redevelopment or rehabilitation or code enforcement, for example. Essential social and economic supportive strategies were usually given only lip service and were rarely integrated with the ongoing or contemplated housing activity. Neighborhood preservation, in contrast, stresses a comprehensive attack on both housing problems and the physical, social, and economic restraints to achieving neighborhood rejuvenation.

One of preservation's major breakthroughs is its flexibility— that is, its application of various groupings and levels of supportive strategies as deemed appropriate by local conditions. This pragma-

FIGURE 1

Rehabilitation and Preservation

	Rehabilitation	Neighborhood Preservation
Differences		
Application	Tool	Program
Focus	Micro; project focus	Macro; focuses on broader environmental forces
Orientation	Physical	Physical, social, and economic
Range/flexibility	Limited to different levels of renovation	Broad spectrum of strategies to address different needs
Public input	Usually one-shot	An on-going process
Track record	Mixed	Advocated but largely not effected
Similarities		
Philosophy	Recycling	Recycling
Policy focus	Housing renovation	Rehabilitation is fundamental
Spatial focus	Urban	Urban

Source: David Listokin and Peter Morris, Neighborhood Preservation and Housing Rehabilitation (New Brunswick, N.J.: Rutgers University Center for Urban Policy Research, forthcoming).

tism contrasts with the dogmatism of past programs, in which one or
a narrow range of remedies was applied under all conditions.

Another difference is that past housing efforts often assumed that
a one-time infusion of aid would be sufficient and would nurture itself
without further assistance. For example, the Section 235 program assumed that a federal write-down for low-income homeownership would
itself be sufficient to stabilize deteriorating urban neighborhoods—a
belief that subsequently proved to be unfounded. Neighborhood preservation, in contrast, accepts the need for long-term supportive strategies, albeit of a changing magnitude as neighborhood conditions themselves evolve.

APPLYING THE NEIGHBORHOOD
PRESERVATION STRATEGY

One of the first steps in the application of a neighborhood preservation strategy is to delineate and classify different neighborhoods on
the basis of their housing quality and general environmental stability.
This is not a new endeavor, and past delineation/classification efforts
might prove useful (see Figure 2).

The next step is to consider the broad range of housing and socioeconomic supportive efforts that could help stabilize physical and
social deterioration. A recent study by the Real Estate Research
Corporation and the Rutgers University Center for Urban Policy Research considered the following strategies:

1. Housing rehabilitation
2. Code enforcement
3. Focused public services
4. Management of abandonment
5. Historic preservation
6. City-neighborhood growth management
7. Comprehensive programs (combining two or more of the
above efforts)

The last and crucial stage is to apply those supportive efforts
deemed most applicable to the different neighborhoods. The same
strategy would be effected in different areas, but to varying degrees.
For example, "gut" rehabilitation could be applied in better-quality
neighorhoods while "cosmetic" renovation may be a more appropriate
holding pattern approach in more deteriorated areas. A careful and
realistic matching of neighborhood conditions and supportive strategies
is the heart of neighborhood preservation. Increasingly, the stress
has been on optimizing extant resources, present occupants, and onsite support structures of schools, stores, churches, and the like.

FIGURE 2

Neighborhood Quality/Stability Classifications: A Summary of Selected Past Efforts

Study/Author	Date	Categories/Stages of Neighborhood Quality/Stability			
		Highest quality / Most stable →	Neighborhood Transition: Stable →	Middle-aged or Conservation →	Worst housing quality / Least stable
U.S. Urban Redevelopment Agency	1944	Development →	Stable →		Clearance
Cleveland Regional Association	1947	Protection →	Conservation →		Rebuilding
Jack Siegal and C. William Brooks	1953	Conservation →	Rehabilitation →		Redevelopment
Raymond Vernon and Edgar M. Hoover	1962	Development →	Conservation (Minor Medium Major) →	Rehabilitation →	Redevelopment
New York City	1968	Initial Development → Early evidence of building and neighborhood deterioration; Building deterioration structures	Transition → Building deterioration (mixed substantial and obsolete structures and neighborhood deficiencies); Building deterioration and dilapidation (substantial structures)	Downgrading → Building deterioration (substantial structures and neighborhood deficiencies); Building deterioration and dilapidation (obsolete structures)	Thinning out → Renewal; Building dilapidation and deterioration (obsolete structures and neighborhood deficiencies); Building dilapidation (frame structures)
Public Affairs Counseling	1973	Healthy and usable →	Incipient decline →	Decline clearly under way → Accelerating decline →	Nonviable and abandoned

Source: David Listokin and Peter Morris, Neighborhood Preservation and Housing Rehabilitation (New Brunswick, N.J.: Rutgers University Center for Urban Policy Research, forthcoming).

FINANCING NEIGHBORHOOD PRESERVATION

Multiple sources are available for the financing of a neighborhood preservation program. Community development block grants
authorized by the 1974 Housing and Community Development Act can
be used for many of the housing and socially supportive efforts that
neighborhood preservation comprises. Recently released program
regulations* declare that the grants can be utilized for the "conservation and expansion of the nation's housing stock" and explicitly authorize
expenditures of discretionary funds for housing rehabilitation, code
enforcement, improvement of public service, and historic preservation. Section 8 of the act provides long-range subsidies for both rehabilitation and new construction. The block grants and Section 8
subsidies are the principal federal financial aids for neighborhood
preservation efforts.

States and localities are also beginning to flex their housing program muscles. This is in part due to growing federal aid for state
and local housing supports provided under the act and revenue sharing.
States and localities are also beginning to realize that they must tailor
housing assistance to the special needs and aspirations of their citizens
and that they have a range of options for doing so. These programs
are outlined in Figures 3 and 4. Many of these subsidies can be used
to finance neighborhood preservation programs, both explicitly and
implicitly. The New Jersey rehabilitation aids, for example, are
viewed by state officials as crucial supports for local neighborhood
conservation efforts. The Neighborhood Housing Services Program is
designed to preserve and improve "gray" areas in Pittsburgh and
other cities. These subsidies, coupled with the emerging federal
aids, are designed to provide the financial wherewithal for neighborhood preservation.

NEIGHBORHOOD PRESERVATION AND
RELIGIOUS ORGANIZATIONS

Religious organizations can play a multiple role in the neighborhood preservation process. Their presence and range of activities
can sometimes aid in the demarcation of separate neighborhoods; a
parish, for example, may have the physical and social cohesion to
constitute a distinct neighborhood. Such organizations and institutions
can provide insight into the supportive housing and socioeconomic
strategies needed to stabilize an area and their effectiveness. This

---

*See Federal Register 39, no. 238 (December 10, 1974), part 2.

FIGURE 3

Evolving State Rehabilitation and Neighborhood Preservation Financing Strategies

Financing Strategy	Some States Using or Contemplating Using Strategy	Advantages	Disadvantages
Allowing municipalities to issue bonds to finance rehabilitation	California, Minnesota, Maryland, New York, Kentucky	1. Expands local potential; in some areas (i.e., California) local bond financing or rehabilitation has been impeded by statutory restrictions or doubts	1. Some municipalities (i.e., New York City) may be overextended in terms of their bond refinancing 2. Tax-exempt bonds raise questions of equity 3. Tax exempts currently have fairly high interest rates
State housing finance agencies (SHFAs) issuing for rehabilitation	Massachusetts and Minnesota are the prime examples	1. SHFAs have a very successful track record, albeit they focus on new construction	1. Bond rating doubt because of "moral pledge" instead of full faith and credit 2. See 2 above 3. See 3 above 4. SHFA disinclination to finance rehabilitation
Direct state bond issues for rehabilitation	Maryland (Maryland Home Financing Program)	1. States have financed a multitude of activities through bond sales 2. Low present cost for state 3. Avoids many of the problems found with SHFA bond rehabilitation financing	1. See 2 above 2. See 3 above
Budgetary financing	New Jersey, Pennsylvania, California	1. Not dependent on vagaries of bond financing	1. With deep subsidy, can be extremely expensive
Insuring private rehabilitation loans	Maryland, New York, Wisconsin	1. High multiplier of state funds	1. May succeed in encouraging more private financing, but does not address problem of subsidizing loans. 2. Actuarial risk hard to determine

Sources: George Sternlieb et al., "An Evaluation of Urban Housing Problems and Programs," report submitted to the New Jersey State Department of Community Affairs, January 1975, by Rutgers University Center for Urban Policy Research; and U.S. Department of Housing and Urban Development, Examples of Local and State Financing of Property Rehabilitation (Washington, D.C.: U.S. Government Printing Office, 1974).

FIGURE 4

Evolving Local Rehabilitation and Neighborhood Preservation Financing Strategies

Financing Strategy	Local Units of Some Governments Using or Contemplating Using Strategy	Advantages	Disadvantages
Budgetary financing	Provo, Utah; Montgomery County, Maryland	1. Not dependent on vagaries of bond market	1. With deep subsidy, can be very expensive
Insuring private rehabilitation loans	New York City; Fresno, California; Clearwater, Florida	1. High multiplier of local funds	1. Actuarial base may be too small 2. May succeed in encouraging more private financing but not address problems of subsidizing loans
Bond sales	Baltimore; New York City; Cincinnati; San Francisco	1. Localities have financed a multitude of activities through bond sales 2. Tax exempt bonds attract investors with little local tax loss 3. Low present local cost	1. Tax exempts currently have fairly high interest rates (this may be a special problem for locality with a poor bond rating) 2. Raises questions of equity
Private-public "two-tier" arrangement	Norfolk, Richmond; Portsmouth, Virginia; Philadelphia; Seattle	1. Interject public agency's credit between homeowner and bank; this reduces financing costs and encourages more private rehabilitation lending	1. Relies on local bank's willingness to make loans
Neighborhood Housing Service (NHS)	Pittsburgh; Washington, D.C.; Cincinnati	1. Cooperative approach to solving problems; has had considerable success in Pittsburgh	1. Depends on foundation support,* which may not always be available or may take considerable time to arrange

*The NHS program is currently receiving federal assistance.

Sources: George Sternlieb et al., "An Evaluation of Urban Housing Problems and Programs," report submitted to the New Jersey State Department of Community Affairs, January 1975, by Rutgers University Center for Urban Policy Research; and U.S. Department of Housing and Urban Development, Examples of Local and State Financing of Property Rehabilitation (Washington, D.C.: U.S. Government Printing Office, 1974).

grass roots input and feedback is an integral part of the neighborhood preservation strategy.

Religious organizations and institutions can also play a role in the implementation of the preservation process. To illustrate, they can sponsor rehabilitation efforts and day care centers, and have done so, and they have provoked such services as family and employment counseling—all of which are essential preservation activities. The very fact that religious organizations and institutions deem it appropriate to remain in declining neighborhoods may in itself constitute a psychological boost to property owners, tenants, and other crucial local institutions, such as local banks.

Religious organizations and institutions have already assumed some of these roles. The Greater Hartford Council of Churches, for example, has participated in Housing Now, Inc., a preservation effort in Hartford designed to stabilize neighborhoods in the city by stimulating homeownership and offering counseling and other services. Other groups have taken similar actions. Their effectiveness will be enhanced in the future if they are coordinated and structured within a neighborhood preservation framework. These phrases are easily said, but their operational difficulties are all too frequently underestimated. Nonprofit corporations are in bad repute. A track record of bankruptcies, inadequate operations, and underestimated costs have left government at all levels increasingly wary. This is not an area in which enthusiasm can replace constant, painstaking administration. Bookkeeping without insight and without true commitment of spirit as well as of time is sterile, but it is nevertheless an essential complement of these virtues.

There are enormous gaps in the web of services that desperately need filling, which is something that religious organizations in all of their manifestations are uniquely capable of providing. One need only look at the opportunities and problems of providing a decent environment and infrastructure for the elderly as an example. Here we have an area that has been the subject of strong support in terms of housing funding and legislation. The gaps, however, between the "housing for the elderly" project, the nursing home (that terrible euphemism), and the chronic care facility must be filled. Can religious organizations begin to package the kind of care that is needed? And if they cannot—then who will?

But again, it is not enough to have enthusiasm unless it is coupled with professional competence. The satire of the nonprofit corporation as "six bewildered preachers and a hotshot lawyer" cannot be tolerated. We are now faced with a decline in the classic modular household. Whether it be the elderly, the single-parent household, or any of the other permutations that depart from the conventional American family, each requires insight, care—and good bookkeeping.

With all of this, we still face the reality of the crumbling neighborhood in an America that is no longer as rich as it was once thought to be.

NEIGHBORHOOD PRESERVATION: SOME DISTURBING ISSUES

Neighborhood preservation offers numerous advantages over past housing programs. Two disturbing issues, however, are likely to accompany such a strategy and therefore deserve mention. First is the question, neighborhood preservation for whom? Past conservation efforts in Georgetown, Washington, D.C.; Brooklyn Heights, New York; and other areas have indeed stabilized the areas, but, at the same time, they have forced lower-income residents and tenants to move. By its very success, preservation will often cause displacement, and this will have adverse social and political repercussions.

The second issue concerns the treatment of the most deteriorated neighborhoods. Many emerging neighborhood preservation strategies tend to either write off many blighted areas or relegate to them only "holding pattern" supportive programs; resources are more often than not focused on transitional "gray neighborhoods." Such a policy may indeed represent an optimal strategy from a cost-benefit perspective, but do we want to abandon portions of the city? Can this be done without serious social and political repercussion?

4

HOW TO UTILIZE AND IMPROVE FEDERAL AND STATE HOUSING PROGRAMS FOR THE ELDERLY

HOW BIG IS THE PROBLEM?

Consider the following extracts from the Senate Report on Developments in Aging: 1973 and January to March 1974 (the "elderly" will be defined here as those who are 65 and over):

- Between 1900 and 1970, the total population of the United States grew almost three times while the older population grew almost seven times—and it is still growing.
- Every day, 4,000 Americans celebrate their 65th birthday and 3,000 of them die, making a net increase of 1,000 per day, or 365,000 elderly per year, at present population levels.
- Most of the elderly (62 percent) are under 75 years of age. Half are just under 73. More than one-third (36 percent) are under 70.
- Between 1960 and 1973, the population of those aged 65 through 74 increased 20 percent, but the population of those aged 75 and over increased 46 percent.
- There are 1.6 million people aged 85 or older.
- Of the elderly 81 percent get along well on their own.
- The median income of elderly persons living alone or with nonrelatives is $2,397, or just under $200 per month.
- The mean rents paid for HUD-assisted housing units for the elderly are $42.95 for rent supplement projects (federal rent subsidy for difference between 25 percent of income and economic rent); $44.06 for public housing units (resident's rent based on percentage of income); and $119.06 for Section 236 projects (with interest subsidy down to 1 percent).
- According to the Bureau of Census, our 1970 population of persons aged 65 and over was over 20 million. It projects 24.1 million in

1980, 27.8 million in 1990, and 28.8 million in the year 2000. If we use the age of 62 to define "elderly," these figures will obviously be substantially greater.

Among the findings of the White House Conference on Aging (1971) was that there was a deficiency of about 1.5 million housing units for the elderly and that each year at least 150,000 new units of specially designed housing for the low-income elderly were needed.

WHAT ARE OUR RESOURCES?

There is a considerable number of elderly persons who have the resources to solve their housing and service needs without special financial assistance. Many private developers have produced condominiums, "Sun Cities," "Leisure Worlds," and so on to meet this market. However, our problem here is with the low-income elderly whose total income would barely pay the rent in a conventionally financed, unsubsidized housing facility for the elderly. These elderly persons must have subsidized rents. The principal source of financing housing for the elderly has been the special programs of HUD. A large amount of housing has been provided with federal assistance over the last 10 to 12 years. However, production has lagged far behind need, as the following table of the number of dwelling units built with HUD assistance to provide sponsors of housing for the elderly indicates:

Program	1972	1973	1974	Inception through September 1974
202	2,006	—	—	44,322
202/236	5,947	1,399	—	27,601
231	775	783	528	42,721
236	5,973	10,223	1,317	34,955
Total	14,701	12,405	1,845	149,599

Figures on the number of dwelling units built with HUD assistance to local housing authorities for housing designed for the elderly are as follows:

1972	1973	1974	Inception through September 1974
19,127	13,214	n.a.	269,234

The total for all units designed for the elderly is thus 418,833.

The Section 202 program will be described in detail later. The Section 202/236 program covers Section 202 applications that have been caught in the termination of the 202 program and processed as a mortgage insurance project under Section 236, but it recognizes as many 202 commitments as possible. This is not available for new applications. The Section 231 program covers mortgage insurance market rate financing of housing for the elderly. This is currently available. The Section 236 program covers mortgage insurance with subsidized interest (down to 1 percent) housing for low-income families. This is not available for new applications.

SECTION 202

The Section 202 program provided for 100 percent direct loans to nonprofit corporations at 3 percent interest for 50 years for the development of housing for the elderly. It was terminated in 1969, presumably because of its impact on the federal budget, and its staff was absorbed into FHA and other agencies.

Under the original 202 program, the loan was made to a special purpose nonprofit corporation, formed by an acceptable sponsor. The sponsor had to provide evidence that at least two lending institutions would not make such a loan to the nonprofit corporation. The sponsor was not legally obligated to the borrower corporation. However, one of the important considerations in loan approval was the evaluation of the sponsor's commitment and capability to develop the project into a successful housing facility for the elderly.

The Section 202 program was administered by a small group of specialists on housing for the elderly. One factor in the success of the 202 program was that these specialists were responsible for the managerial success of the projects as well as for resolving the development problems. There were comparatively few legislative constraints and the administrative procedures allowed them considerable latitude. Furthermore, since it was a federal loan program, the conditions of the loan could be modified if it appeared to be in the best interests of the project, its owners, and the federal government.

Congress has recently acted to revive the 202 program.* However, it is becoming increasingly apparent that HUD has no plans to revive Section 202 as a special program of housing for the elderly.

_____

*This congressional action occurred when the Independent Offices Appropriation Act of 1975 (October 17) appropriated $375 million for permanent loans to the elderly for housing under Section 202.

Apparently, it will be a market interest rate construction loan program, probably expected to roll over every two years. Applications will most likely be handled by established HUD field office processing staff and will have to meet the established FHA minimum property standards and be processed in accordance with FHA underwriting and processing requirements. Although representatives of housing for the elderly will be designated in each office, they will be advisers and will not take part in the review and approval process.

It is understandable that HUD does not want to set up special procedures and special handling for a one-shot program of only $215 million. It is much simpler to absorb it into the existing system. After all, the $215 million made available only after a long battle between the administration and Congress will only fund approximately 8,600 units at $25,000 each or 43 projects of 200 units each. Obviously, this is not what is wanted, but how do we get what is wanted unless the program is made much larger or unless it is expected to be funded again each year?

SECTION 8

The federal government seems to be backing out of funding multifamily housing facilities for the poor and the elderly. It appears to want to get out of the construction business; instead, it prefers to provide income assistance so that the individual can find the living arrangement that meets his needs. Then the government provides a cash supplement to make up the difference between the rent cost and what the individual can afford to pay.

This is basically the Section 8 program of HUD. Essentially, it is a good program and can help hundreds of thousands of poor families. It can also help the elderly. As of April 1975, approximately $900 million dollars had been distributed to the HUD field offices for this program.

The major problem with Section 8 funding is that it is a rent supplement program and cannot cover services. Housing allowances for the elderly should include other essential costs in addition to shelter rent, such as health care, limited housekeeping, and congregate dining areas. Why not consider a major effort to revamp Section 8 so that it can be used to cover the full housing and service needs of the elderly?

RURAL RENTAL HOUSING

The Rural Rental Housing program of the FmHA is becoming increasingly effective for sponsors of housing for the elderly in rural communities.

The FmHA makes insured loans to qualified individuals or organizations to provide rental housing for families and individuals with low and moderate incomes and for senior citizens. Senior citizens are defined as persons 62 years of age or over, and in the case of a married couple, only either the wife or the husband need qualify. Housing financed with these loans must be located in a rural community and designed for independent living. Rural communities include towns with a population of up to 10,000. The Housing and Community Development Act of 1974 authorizes FmHA to make loans in areas with a population of up to 20,000 outside SMSAs, providing the secretaries of HUD and Agriculture determine that a serious lack of mortgage credit exists in such areas.

The payment period is not to exceed 40 years from the date of the note, except for a loan to provide housing for senior citizens only, in which case it is not to exceed 50 years. The current interest rate is 8.5 percent. If the units are occupied by low-income elderly, interest credits that may reduce the interest rate to as low as 1 percent are allowed to the owner, provided this is reflected in reduced rent. Also, the sponsors may be able to obtain a commitment for Section 8 housing allowance payment assistance, which assures that the elderly resident will pay no more than 25 percent of his income for rent. During fiscal year 1973, a total of 3,781 units was provided by FmHA for senior citizens. In fiscal year 1974, a total of 4,394 units was provided for senior citizens.

HUD MORATORIUM

Since the devastating moratorium that stopped the FHA programs, there has not been any substantial amount of federally assisted new housing. Instead, there has been increasing support for housing allowance payments, first under Section 23 and now under the Section 8 Housing Assistance Payments Program (that is, rent supplements).

To further complicate the problem, there has been much discussion about the question of whether housing for the elderly is a problem that warrants special treatment. Those supporting a strong program of housing and related facilities for the elderly include nonprofit provider organizations representing over 20 million elderly. The Federal government probably prefers to consider the housing needs of the elderly as an element of the total housing needs of the poor.

However, as HUD has cut back its financial assistance for housing construction, it has encouraged and provided considerable housing allowance payments assistance to both local and state housing authorities. Thirty-two states now have their own housing authorities, and most of them are empowered to sell tax-free bonds and are able to

make loans to sponsors of housing for the elderly at below-market interest rates. HUD provides them with an allocation of Section 8 rent
assistance funds and gives the state considerable latitude in administering these funds. Under present circumstances, this may be one of
the best routes to go for new housing facilities.

WHAT ARE WE DOING WRONG ?

Although the various organizations, the administration, and the
Congress have for years acknowledged the need for housing and services for the elderly, virtually no housing legislation that benefits the
nonprofit organizations has been recently enacted. In fact, the benefits of some previously enacted legislation have been terminated, such
as the original 202 program. This has been done not just by one administration, but by both Republican and Democratic administrations.
We must ask ourselves what is wrong with what we are attempting to
do.

The need for housing and services for the elderly touches us
personally as well as professionally, since most of us have family
members who are senior citizens. However, in spite of the fact that
we are involved in the problem and can become emotional over it, we
cannot seem to find the combination that enables the nonprofit organizations to produce an adequate supply of housing and services for the
elderly at prices they can afford.

If we have a good case for our efforts to obtain federal financial
assistance for special facilities for the elderly, we obviously are not
making an effective presentation to the administration and the Congress.

Most of our programs are based on the age of 62 as being the
age when we all become "elderly." By this definition, I am a senior
citizen, yet I am in good health, work full-time, maintain an active
family life, and enjoy sports. I certainly do not feel like a senior
citizen or elderly, and I am sure that there are many other people
who do not like being categorized as such.

Why not consider changing the age for the purpose of being eligible for special housing to 70 or 75? This would reduce the number
of elderly eligible for special housing by at least one-third. With increased longevity, a good case for such a change can be made. With
an elderly population eligible for special housing reduced to a more
manageable size and comprising persons who are more likely to require special facilities, we might find less resistance in seeking special assistance from Congress.

Are we on the right track in our efforts to obtain financial assistance to meet the housing needs of the elderly? Each year we have
to fight for every little bit of assistance we get and never have enough
to meet our needs.

Is it being realistic to depend so heavily on federal financial assistance to provide housing for the elderly? Should private sources be more heavily involved? Should the community provide more support?

Almost everyone would agree that the problems of the elderly are problems of the community, not of religious and other benevolent organizations. Although these groups have sponsored projects as a service to the community, very often only 15 to 20 percent of the residents of the facility or project belong to the sponsoring organization. Yet we expect the sponsoring group to contribute heavily to the cost of the project and to also provide additional operating funds as well as many hours of voluntary service. This might not be an equitable solution to providing housing and services to the elderly.

The sponsors involved in nonprofit projects usually have a board made up of community leaders. The sponsor is represented on the board but will not necessarily dominate it. Other basic characteristics of the sponsor are: little or no money; no real credit; very limited authority to enter into long-term contracts; probably no paid, full-time staff to deal with housing problems; a deep interest in the elderly in its community; and a commitment to work on a volunteer basis to meet the needs of the elderly.

Sponsors of nonprofit housing for the elderly should make a special effort to obtain strong cosponsors. Why shouldn't religious and social welfare organizations begin to look for cosponsors that have great financial strength and at the same time recognize an obligation to the elderly and the community?

A few years ago, some of the largest corporations in the country were exploring the possibility of building housing for the elderly. Why not revive this interest? Why not use them as cosponsors? Why shouldn't the nation's largest employers share in the problem solving for their retirees? They have used the good years of the elderly; they should help out during the tough ones. This would not change the nonprofit character of the projects, but it would be another way of helping to solve the problem of providing housing and services needs for the elderly.

PROJECT FACILITIES AS COMMUNITY
SERVICE CENTERS

We have participated in providing hundreds of homes for the elderly, each one designed and operated as a separate, self-contained entity. However, a number of housing facilities have been constructed that included multipurpose "senior centers." Programs have been developed within these facilities that are available to the nonresi-

dent elderly in the community. Shouldn't this concept be brought into
sharp focus and greatly expanded?

We know that in every community there are countless elderly
who will never have the opportunity to live in a well-planned and well-
operated facility for the elderly. Should we begin to think of special
projects for the elderly as a core of services to the elderly in the environs? Should the city, the county, the state, and the federal government expand their financial assistance for such projects to permit an
adequate senior center with food, health care, day care, recreation,
and so on? This might permit many elderly to remain in their present,
less-than-satisfactory living situation and thus ease the need for
specially designed housing. Perhaps the city can be persuaded to
more vigorously assist nonprofit organizations in developing and operating such centers in order to relieve the city of a tremendous housing
responsibility.

WHERE DO WE GO FROM HERE?

Are the housing needs of the elderly being met on an equitable
basis? The administration will say "yes" because of the Section 8
housing allowance program. They contend that a large proportion of
Section 8 funds will go to the elderly.

I would say "no," because the elderly need a large volume of
housing designed to meet their special needs and operated as nonprofit
facilities by sponsors dedicated to serving the elderly. A housing allowance (or rent supplement) does not meet this need.

Conscientious sponsoring organizations might combine their
efforts to bring about the following changes:

1. Obtain additional Section 202 appropriations so that the program will be large enough to substantially contribute toward meeting
the housing need;

2. Persuade the secretary of HUD to reexamine the regulations
and instructions relating to Section 202 in order to produce a direct
loan program similar to the original 202 rather than restrict it to a
construction loan program;

3. Establish an effective working relationship with all of the
state housing agencies in order to obtain a fair share of the assistance
available to them and to influence their rules and regulations so that
they will be more responsive to your needs;

4. Seek additional financial assistance in order to develop
existing and new projects into community service or core facilities to
serve the elderly in the environs;

5. Reexamine the age distinctions for the elderly so that we can provide more effectively for the older elderly (age 70 or 75 and over) who must have special living facilities;

6. Initiate carefully planned campaigns to involve big business as cosponsors of nonprofit housing facilities for the elderly, recognizing that we cannot hope to get as much federal financial assistance for housing as is needed;

7. Rework the Section 8 program so that it can be more responsive in meeting the housing and service costs of the elderly;

8. Recognize the importance of a team effort in obtaining more or improved benefits for the elderly.

5

HOW TO DEVELOP CREATIVE PUBLIC HOUSING COMMUNITIES FOR LOW-INCOME PEOPLE THROUGH CONVENTIONAL AND LEASED PROGRAMS

The words "public housing" conjure up a variety of images. Most people tend to think of monster high-rise projects and might remember pictures of the dynamiting of one of the largest of these projects several years ago in St. Louis.

In reality, with few exceptions it can be said that there is no such thing as wholly private housing in this country. Almost all housing is regulated, and a great deal of housing is assisted in one way or another by government at the local, state, and federal level.

At the other extreme, there is also no such thing as wholly public housing, in the sense of being government housing. That is, there is no housing that is financed solely by government funds, built solely by government employees, and operated solely by government entities.

Thus, there is no clear distinction between public and private housing in this country, and the use of either term without qualification is usually misleading.

LOCAL, STATE, AND FEDERAL HOUSING PROGRAMS

While local and state governments regulate and influence the pattern of housing development either by direct measures—such as zoning and subdivision controls—or by indirect measures, almost all housing assistance depends in some degree—often entirely—on the federal government.

The major federal housing program, as measured in dollar volume, is housing subsidy for single-family homeownership. This subsidy, however, is provided neither by HUD nor by FmHA. Instead, it is provided through the tax system in the form of a "tax expenditure."

A tax expenditure, or tax subsidy, is the amount that the Internal Revenue Service does not collect because of some provision of the tax laws. (Most people refer to tax expenditures that they do not like as "loopholes.")

The Office of Management and Budget estimates that for fiscal year 1976, federal tax expenditures for owner-occupied housing will amount to $11.3 billion. In 1970, they were about $6 billion, and in 1973 they were $7.9 billion.

The increase in tax expenditures since 1973 is $1 billion more than estimated 1976 federal outlays for all subsidized programs for low- and moderate-income people combined. (Direct outlays for low- and moderate-income housing subsidy programs in 1976 are estimated at $2.5 billion.) These tax expenditures go primarily to middle- and upper-income people. Furthermore, these subsidies, if ended, would have to be replaced by another subsidy program in order to avoid foreclosures or sacrifice of other basic essentials, at least for families with incomes of between $10,000 and, perhaps, $30,000.

Few people realize how inequitable these tax subsidies really are. In 1973—the most recent year for which information is available—for example, the average tax subsidy for households with incomes below $3,000 claiming this deduction was $23. At the other extreme, the average subsidy for homeowners with incomes above $100,000 was $2,449.

Unlike other housing subsidies, tax subsidies are not subject to annual review or to the budgetary process. Nor are they subject to administrative actions, such as the freeze that has cut off new subsidized housing programs since 1973. Instead, they are available as a matter of right to all who claim them on their tax returns. In 1973, 25 million American families benefited from these tax subsidies. Moreover, only one-quarter go to people with incomes below $15,000. More than half go to people with incomes above $20,000.

In contrast, there are fewer than 3 million families receiving the more publicized housing subsidies of HUD and FmHA. About a million are in public housing. In 1976, the cost of these subsidies is estimated to be about $2.5 billion. This is about $1 billion less than the increase in tax subsidies between 1973 and 1976. Moreover, this includes all the subsidized units ever built since the beginning of subsidized housing programs during the depression years of the 1930s.

HOUSING SUBSIDIES AND HOUSING NEEDS

It is useful to compare the level of housing subsidy programs with estimates of housing need. While these estimates vary with the point of view of the estimator, a few bench-mark numbers may be

useful. In 1968, the Congress estimated this need over the 10-year
period between 1968 and 1978 at 6 million subsidized units and 20 million unsubsidized units, using as a basis for its action a careful study
done by a special committee appointed by President Johnson. These
specific housing goals were embodied in the Housing and Urban Development Act of 1968. The 6-million-unit goal was based on replacing
the seriously substandard housing then in existence.

In 1974, the Joint Center for Urban Study of the Massachusetts
Institute of Technology and Harvard University, under a contract with
HUD, estimated the need for subsidized housing units at approximately
13 million. HUD itself, in its report Housing for the Seventies, estimated that there were at least 15 million families eligible, according
to their incomes, for housing subsidies for whom there was no subsidized housing available. HUD's breakdown of these families shows
that there were 1.5 million households with incomes below $1,000;
3.1 million households with incomes between $1,000 and $2,000; 3.6
million households with incomes between $3,000 and $4,000; and 3.1
million households with incomes between $4,000 and $5,000.

There is the view in some quarters that low-income people live
in poor housing because of poor budget practices or because they are
spending their income for other purposes. This is simply not true.
Again using HUD's figures from Housing for the Seventies, we find
that households with incomes below $2,000 were spending almost two-
thirds of their incomes for rent (64 percent); households with incomes
between $2,000 and $3,000 were spending 52 percent of their incomes
for rent; households with incomes between $3,000 and $4,000 were
spending almost one-third (32 percent) of their income for rent;
households with incomes between $4,000 and $5,000 were spending
more than one-quarter (27 percent) of their incomes for rent; and
households with incomes between $5,000 and $6,000 were spending
22 percent of their incomes for rent. Thus, the lower one's income,
the more one spends for housing.

                         HOUSING PRODUCTION

Subsidized housing production reached its peak in 1972, just before the freeze on subsidized programs imposed by administrative
fiat in January 1973. In 1972, two-thirds of all new housing production was priced to serve families with incomes above $10,000. Only
3 percent served families with incomes below $4,000. Had these
rates been continued, it would have taken 14 years to build new houses
for the 25 million families with incomes above $10,000, but it would
have taken 179 years to provide new housing for the 15 million families
with incomes below $4,000. By the end of 1974, when the impact of

the moratorium had largely been felt, it would have taken more than 300 years to provide a new house for every family with an income below $4,000.

As population has grown, so have housing needs. If low- and moderate-income families are to be confined to the existing housing stock—as they will be unless new subsidized housing is provided—they will be forced to live in either center cities, the older suburbs, or the built-up rural areas. New housing construction is, and has been, mainly suburban. Indeed, housing is the major reason for the geographical segregation that the Kerner Commission characterized almost a decade ago as leading to "two societies, one black and one white, separate and unequal." As long as housing remains segregated, it will be difficult to integrate employment, education, or other aspects of American life. Housing can only be desegregated if people have access to new housing in newly developing areas without regard to their race or income.

THE PUBLIC HOUSING PROGRAM

Public housing had its beginnings during the early years of the depression of the 1930s as a public works program.

Housing is a major source of employment. According to Bureau of Labor statistics, each new housing unit provides 1.67 work-years of onsite and offsite employment. There are indirect effects of this employment as well, which means that one can calculate conservatively that each additional housing unit creates approximately two jobs.

While housing conditions in the 1930s were perhaps as bad as they are now, the major reason for the federal government's beginning a housing program was to provide jobs. The program was successful, and the United States Housing Act of 1937 established the public housing program on a permanent basis. Interestingly enough, employment was still the primary consideration; the declaration of policy described the purpose of the act as being "to alleviate present and recurring unemployment and to remedy the unsafe and unsanitary housing conditions and the acute shortage of decent, safe and sanitary dwellings for families of low income."

In this time of critical unemployment—with official estimates that 5.5 percent of the labor force will be unemployed in 1980 even if all goes well—it is worth remembering that housing can contribute more immediately to remedying unemployment than perhaps any other program or economic activity.

During the depression, the federal government made a brief effort to construct public housing directly. This activity was challenged in the courts, and a lower court decision preventing this was not appealed. As a result, the public housing program has, until recently, been channeled through local public housing agencies and has therefore rested on state and local government approval of the undertakings. Since many communities do not welcome low-income people, they exclude low-income housing.

The public housing provided during the 1930s was, by and large, satisfactory in quality, though it fell far short in quantity of meeting housing needs. Housing construction, except for war housing, was virtually suspended during World War II. As the war drew to a close and postwar planning began, housing was a major consideration.

Proposals for substantial public housing construction, along with slum clearance, received widespread support. Senator Robert Taft of Ohio, who was known as "Mr. Republican," was a major proponent of public housing, as were Senators Robert F. Wagner and Allen J. Ellender on the Democratic side. Efforts were made prior to the end of the war to pass legislation providing both for slum clearance and substantial public housing construction. These efforts culminated in 1949 in the passage of the Wagner-Ellender-Taft Bill, which authorized the construction of one million public housing units over a 10-year period. Its premise was that 10 percent of all new housing construction should be public housing.

The stimulus provided by the Housing Act of 1949 resulted in the construction of a series of monster high-rise public housing projects in urban areas, where sites were not available on vacant land. The construction of these high-rise public housing projects resulted from a curious aversion to "double subsidies."

The 1949 act, in addition to providing for public housing, also provided for redevelopment, or slum clearance. Subsidies were available to cover the difference between the cost of land acquired by local public agencies and the value of the land after the slum housing on it had been cleared. However, only a few cities provided slum sites for public housing, the notion being that one subsidy—the land write-down—was enough and to add the public housing construction subsidy to this was inappropriate and unwise. The result was that exorbitantly high land costs (the cost of acquisition under generally prevailing practice was based on the capitalized income from the slum properties, not on an assessment of their physical value) coupled with the limitation on cost for public housing construction meant that the only feasible way to provide public housing in inner city areas was to build high-rise, high-density projects.

No one favored such projects. The records of the time are replete with the recognition that high-rise public housing does not provide suitable housing for low-income people, particularly for families with children. The decision faced by local housing agencies, however, was whether to provide high-rise public housing or no public housing at all.

These remarks apply only to large cities. A great deal of public housing was provided in small towns. These and some city projects were low-rise, often single-family, houses, attractive to their residents and a boon to the surrounding communities. By and large, they have had none of the problems commonly associated with public housing.

THE 1950s AND 1960s AND PUBLIC HOUSING

The 1950s was a decade of retrenchment. It was also another chapter in the era of a search for a cheap and painless solution to low-income housing problems. The proposal was advanced that, if only we could take exorbitant profits out of slum property and provide rehabilitation, no subsidies would be necessary to provide decent housing for low-income people. The notion of urban renewal and neighborhood conservation was born, and new public housing construction was limited to fewer than the number of units needed to provide for low-income families whose homes had been torn down for urban renewal, code enforcement, or federal highway construction.

The 1960s was a decade of experimentation and innovation in public housing. Increasingly, not only community groups but public housing authorities recognized that high-rise projects were a cure worse than the disease. Housing authorities proposed a variety of alternatives: the leasing of existing units from private landlords; the purchase of existing units and their operation as public housing rather than building new projects; and asking private builders to construct housing to public housing standards and then buying the projects. In addition, for the first time, tenants were named to the boards of some housing authorities.

Even during the 1960s, housing authority boards were overwhelmingly composed of real estate and business people, with a smattering of people from social welfare backgrounds—but no tenants. The operation of public housing thus tended to be paternalistic and unresponsive to tenant needs. Gradually this changed, and some housing authorities began to encourage the formation of tenant unions. Tenant unions in other housing authorities were organized in spite of management opposition. A growing number of housing authorities recognized the importance of tenant membership on their board of directors and tenant input into decision making. However, it was not until the late 1960s—30 years or more after the program began—that public housing evolved to the point where it could be truly responsive to both tenant and community needs.

OCCUPANCY CHANGES AND OPERATING COSTS
IN PUBLIC HOUSING

While these changes in public housing itself were evolving, there were companion changes occurring in the occupancy. During the 1930s, when public housing was born, public housing tenants were largely the working poor. During the 1950s and early 1960s, when public housing expanded greatly as a result of the Housing Act of 1949, we were in a period of relatively adequate housing supply and relatively full employment. Almost any white family with a regularly employed wage earner could purchase adequate, though modest, housing. The result was that public housing became increasingly attractive only to economic dropouts, that is, people who had no regular jobs and no housing opportunities other than public housing.

This had an important impact on the public housing program. The public housing subsidy as provided in both the 1937 and 1949 acts was limited to a construction subsidy, though a cumbersome one.

So-called annual contributions covered the interest and amortization on 40-year bonds floated in the private market and used to finance the construction of public housing projects. There were no subsidies available for operating costs. Over the years, operating costs began to rise, and housing authorities increasingly coped with this either by charging their tenants a disproportionate share (over 20 percent) of their incomes or by excluding very-low-income people from public housing.

By 1969 this situation had become so severe that legislative action was necessary, and the Brooke-Sparkman amendments were added to basic housing legislation. These amendments limited the amount that tenants could be charged to not more than 20 percent of their incomes and provided federal operating subsidies to cover the deficits that would thereby occur. It was not until after adoption and implementation of these amendments that public housing for the first time became truly available to low-income families at rents that they could afford.

Few, however, were willing to face up to the full implications of the amendments. Adequate housing simply costs a great deal more than low-income people can pay. Part of the cost is for the structure itself. Part is for its maintenance and operation. In recent years, these maintenance and operating costs have risen dramatically. Fuel costs, for example, have more than doubled in many areas. The result of these rising operating costs and the reluctance of the federal government to make the subsidies available was to force housing authorities to do two things: first, to cut back on maintenance and services and, second, to try to exclude low-income families so as to obtain higher rents. Thus, the physical problems of many public hous-

ing projects caused by their high-rise, high-density nature were compounded by problems of adequate maintenance and funds for operation.

The federal government was not helpful at this juncture. The
Office of Management and Budget sought to impound public housing
operating funds. George Romney, then secretary of HUD, warned
glumly of "runaway" costs of housing subsidy programs and suggested
that state and local governments foot part of the bill. Public housing
itself got a bad name and was unwelcome not only in neighborhoods
where poor people were excluded but in low-income neighborhoods as
well.

SECTIONS 235 AND 236 PROGRAMS

Meanwhile, the federal government was undertaking other forms
of subsidy programs. These included a direct-loan program at an interest rate of about 3 percent for housing for the elderly (the 202
program). Then, in 1968, with the adoption of the 6-million-subsidized-
housing-unit goal, came two new programs, under which the government
subsidized the difference between the market interest rate and an effective interest rate of as low as 1 percent. The sales program is
known as Section 235 and the rental program as Section 236.

In part because of the nature of a tax shelter, Section 236 became
particularly attractive for limited dividend investors, and thousands of
units were built. Again, as with public housing, the subsidy went only
to the cost of providing the structure, and not to its operation. Moreover, the subsidy was "shallow," covering only the interest costs and
not the principal. Thus, neither 235 nor 236 was able to serve low-
income families. Rather, they and their companion programs in the
FmHA—known as Sections 502 and 515—provided shelter for moderate-
income families.

In part these interest subsidy programs were a reflection of the
desire of the federal government to not add large capital expenditures
to the federal budget. This is because the so-called unified federal
budget, projected first in 1967 and actually adopted in 1969, lists total
amounts and does not distinguish between one-time capital expenditures
or investments and operating expenditures or carrying charges. Therefore, it became politically attractive to minimize annual costs. Thus,
even though the total interest costs over the life of a 40-year mortgage
would be at least twice the mortgage amount, federal policy makers
chose to make these interest subsidy payments. Direct federal loans,
such as those provided under the 202 program, would have been cheaper
in the long run, although they would have looked larger in the federal
budget each year.

The nature of the tax shelter, which was primarily through accelerated depreciation or writing off the investment during its early years, was such as to give limited dividend owners little stake in the long-term viability of developments. This was to prove to be the undoing of the 236 program. The 235 program for homeowners had different problems, the primary one being that in many cities unscrupulous owners sold existing housing in tumble-down condition to buyers who had few alternatives available.

While opinions differ, most students of subsidized housing programs conclude that the major problems in 235 and 236 were caused by the structure of the programs themselves, that is, they provided only interest subsidies, plus poor administration by HUD. This was, at least in part, because George Romney, the incoming HUD secretary in 1969, was far more interested in pursuing technological innovation than in effectively administering the new subsidy programs provided by the Housing and Urban Development Act of 1968.

The combination of valid criticisms of the shortcomings of a substantial portion of the 235 and 236 housing plus the commitment of the Nixon administration in its second term to withdrawing the federal government from involvement in domestic social programs provided the rationale for a freeze on all additional subsidized housing in early 1973. There is evidence that the decision to terminate the programs came first and the study and evaluation came later. After almost a year of study, the administration gave lukewarm endorsement to housing allowances as a major means of meeting the housing needs of low-income people. Simultaneously, it was revamping the part of the public housing program that called for leasing units from private developers.

LEASING

The leasing program, initiated during the 1960s, was first intended to give housing authorities flexibility in areas with high vacancy rates, so that they could rent vacant units on the private market rather than construct additional units. A number of developers and housing authorities worked out arrangements for the construction and leasing of entire projects under this program.

In 1974, the administration turned to leasing through public housing as its sole approach to subsidized housing. The program, which had been known as Section 23, its original section number as part of the amended Housing Act of 1937, became Section 8 of the revised Housing Act of 1937, as incorporated in the Housing and Community Development Act of 1974. (One of the major difficulties in dealing with housing is the arcane numerology that technicians use to refer to the programs and their transformations.)

The subsidy under regular public housing is a fairly simple one. It covers the interest and amortization on the bonds financing the construction of the project plus some operating subsidies, depending on the incomes and rents paid by tenants. For leased public housing under the old Section 23 program, the subsidy limit was the amount that would have to be paid for new construction. The subsidy itself, however, covered the difference between the tenants' rent and the unsubsidized market rent for the unit.

Section 8 provides a variation of this: tenants pay 15 to 25 percent of their total income for rent, depending on the size, age, and composition of their families and whether or not they have a serious illness or other extraordinary needs. The subsidy makes up the difference between this amount and the "fair market rent," or, in some instances, a somewhat lower rent, if that is determined to be equitable. Section 8 subsidies are available in developments of any type; that is, Section 8 units can be provided by housing authorities, by nonprofit organizations, by limited dividend corporations, by cooperatives, or by for-profit groups. Priority is given to developments in which less than 20 percent of the units are subsidized.

This last provision is a reflection of HUD's desire to eliminate public influence in the provision of housing. The rationale is that if less than one-fifth of the units in any development are subsidized, market constraints will see to it that the housing provided is of high quality, is well maintained, and is a good value for the rent received.

A total of 600,000 units is available through June 1976 under this program. It is highly doubtful, in the opinion of most observers, that these units will actually be provided, although they are available on paper. Moreover, not all of them will be the products of new construction. The Section 8 subsidies can be used for existing housing and for rehabilitation as well as for new building.

The economics of housing make it impossible for anyone to provide adequate housing without subsidy at costs that low- and moderate-income families can afford to pay. This is true of existing housing and even more true of new construction. Indeed, only about one-fifth of all families can afford to live in unsubsidized new construction.

SECTION 8 PROGRAM

Meanwhile, as a result of the freeze, the only housing subsidy available on a major scale is the Section 8 housing assistance payments program in metropolitan areas. Section 8 is also available in nonmetropolitan areas, along with interest credit programs through FmHA.

Thus, all organizations interested in providing subsidized housing should look to the potential of Section 8, but with caution. The Section 8 program provides a monthly subsidy payment. It does not provide for financing of the construction of the housing, which must be done through other means and, in these times, is difficult. However, since it is the only game in town, it is the one to play for those who wish to develop subsidized housing.

THE ROLE OF CHURCHES AND RELATED GROUPS

Most important, particularly in these times, is the role of churches and related groups as advocates of adequate housing programs. The Housing Act of 1949 set the goal of "a decent home and suitable environment for every American family." As already mentioned, some 25 million American families receive housing subsidies through the tax system, compared to fewer than 2.5 million that receive subsidies from other sources. Moreover, those receiving tax subsidies have higher incomes and receive greater subsidies than those living in subsidized housing.

Yet it is widely believed that one major cause of federal deficits are federal housing subsidies on a large scale. In fact, these direct federal subsidies represent only a fraction of 1 percent of the total federal budget. It is inconceivable that people would fail to react if they knew the truth about housing conditions and housing subsidies.

A primary contribution of churches and related groups toward building better communities through the use of public housing is the advocacy of enough public housing in the broader sense: public housing or public subsidies should be available to all who need them, offering freedom of housing choice. Concerned nonprofit groups can make their contribution by developing their own housing. They can also contribute by interpreting the true nature of the housing problem and by acting in their own communities as well as by joining with others to attempt to improve federal housing legislation.

The Reverend Martin Luther King once described 11 o'clock on a Sunday morning as "the most segregated hour in America." The suburban communities and urban neighborhoods that exclude low-income housing are not devoid of churchgoers or people with social concerns. But people need to be informed and provided with opportunities for action. They can then take the initiative by exploring the housing needs of their communities and advocating programs to meet them. A major opportunity exists in communities of 50,000 or more under the community development block grant program. Under this program, each community receiving federal community development funds must evaluate its needs for subsidized housing. If the evaluations are honest, they will show a wide gap between needs and resources. Concerned people can find out about their community needs, see whether they are adequately stated, and then press for the resources to meet them.

There is no magic in public housing. But it does provide a program that can operate through conventional public housing and local public housing agencies to provide adequately designed, built, and maintained housing or through Section 8 in a variety of other ways. And it is the only means that we have right now of beginning to meet our housing needs.

6

MANAGING THE PROJECT

DEVELOPING SENSITIVE MANAGEMENT

The development of sensitive, responsive, and professional management is an important part of the task of providing decent housing. Good management can really be described as humane management directed to a full range of sensitivity for human needs in keeping the promise of decent housing.

The burden of sensitivity falls not only to management but to each and every individual involved in the keeping of the promise of decent housing, from the beginning of the concept to the eventual resident. Sensitivity in management begins where all management must begin—at the inception of the planning process.

This is the first rule for developing management sensitivity and responsiveness—we must begin at the beginning and we must know the costs, both in terms of money and in terms of human acceptance of the proposed facilities. If we do not know these matters and if we are not allowed to communicate them from the beginning, we cannot manage decent housing because it will have been destroyed by the ineptitude of its development as well as of its operation.

Too often management responsibility is given to the management team upon completion of the project. Management is brought into the picture at the wrong time. The date of project completion for management takeover is too late for the development of a sensitive, responsive, and professional program. The harsh realities of day-to-day operation and the multitude of attendant duties make it almost impossible to develop any kind of a management program or plan, much less a sensitive one. And without total involvement in project planning, day-to-day management policies and practices can hardly be termed professional, much less responsive.

HOW GOOD MANAGEMENT OPERATES

The management team, if it does its job and knows its obligations, provides the basic data about human responses and reactions to
the world of multifamily housing. We know the responses to rules and
regulations, maintenance and repair, children and senior citizens,
families without parental guidance, and a host of experiences and per-
ceptions flowing from living and working in housing sponsored by well-
meaning groups that sometimes have little realization of the human
elements that really make housing a home.

How have we acquired this knowledge, which is so necessary to
the planning and development of decent housing as well as to its continuing service and operation?

Management is an art that combines many disciplines, and it is
a combination of many skills. Management is the planning of events
in an orderly manner, and it is a planned means to an end. Management is not merely reaction—it causes things to happen for the benefit
of those by whom and for whom it is employed. It is a never-ending
process. It requires analysis, research, planning, execution, and
the evaluation of results so that plans can be updated, executed again
in light of changed circumstances, and reevaluated based upon the new
results. The program is continuous in its efforts to meet long-term
goals in the light of ever-changing conditions.

Regardless of the academic descriptions of management, the
management process basically involves human elements—those it moti-
vates to serve and those it serves. In order to accomplish its objectives, management must be aware of the individual as well as of the
group, so that social objectives can be met without infringing upon
individual aspirations. Without human awareness and understanding,
the entire process of analysis, planning, execution, and evaluation in
the cycle of management fails to achieve its goals in the long run.

Since management deals with the physical end product, namely,
the housing development, it is qualified to counsel the developers, the
planners, the sponsors, the designers, the financiers, and the
builders about the physical needs that have so often been ignored in
past monuments to our failure to provide really decent housing. However, this counsel will be useless unless the information has been
based upon human response, human need, and human dignity. Physical
facilities and dispassionate operation sow the seeds of failure in our
goal for decent housing and the commitment we make to provide it.

THE SPONSORING AGENCIES

So often, projects are born with complete goodwill and abysmal
misunderstanding. Management can be of aid to the sponsoring agency

by helping to define what are really to be the long-term goals and objectives. Who is to be served, how should they be served, and how
are they being helped today? Are the present service parameters
actually providing the assistance they were designed and conceived to
give, or is the program just another housing project in the most dis-
mal sense of the term? Is the program designed for interim housing
for those moving upward economically or socially or is the program
envisioned to aid those who must remain there virtually a lifetime
because of circumstances beyond their control and their ability to cope?

Only when the real goals and objectives are defined with the
help of those in management who face the daily application and use of
the final program can the sponsor evaluate its own commitment of
resources, time, energy, and frustration. Does the sponsor have the
staying power to really do the job that is required to meet its objectives?
That staying power will be tested many times, not only during the development stages but in the years ahead, when the brick and mortar
are housing the people for whom the project was built.

The management team cannot make the decision of the sponsor.
All it can do is provide advice and counsel, so that the institution can
understand what it is seeking to do and what its obligations are, in
order to provide not only the physical facilities but the long-term commitment of support as well.

MANAGEMENT AND HOUSING DESIGN

Management counsel has a place in the design program of the
housing. Often, accommodations are designed on the basis of what the
architect or the engineer perceives as the need. We cannot fault this
approach, because how can the architect or the engineer get to know
the real needs unless management provides the intelligence data essential to building a development that can be operated and used for the
benefit of those for whom it is intended? Architects and engineers
also tend to be product oriented—they view equipment and structure
purely from a cost or an artistic viewpoint. Here again, they are
working in their own areas of expertise and there is no fault to assess.
However, the final product must be operable by the management team.
Every aspect of the physical structure and its environment must be
evaluated in terms of its long-term cost of operation. Long-term increased operating costs often turn out to be much more expensive than
they would have been if the right product or correct finish had been
used in the first place.

Initial cost is not the only criterion of project development.
Project costs may well affect the property's ability to support its use
over the long run, thus destroying any savings made initially. Long-

term value must equate to original cost—it cannot be realized unless operational costs are reasonable and manageable.

Once the preliminary plans have been conceptualized, the manager must carefully analyze them in order to initiate a management plan. This starts with a comprehensive critique of the plan so that every corner of the facilities will be evaluated for its ultimate use by a resident. Does the site allow for enjoyment of natural amenities? Is there easy access, or will the plan cause traffic and resident friction? Has the site been properly used and balanced between natural features and the costs of grounds maintenance? What about snow removal, drainage, trees, roads, parking, trash removal, security, lighting, play areas, and passive recreation appearance? The manager must ultimately make the plan work, so the critique must be practical as well as understandable.

How about the residences themselves? What are the sizes? Will they actually be "decent" for the family size for which they are being offered? What about the corridor finish? Can it be maintained in view of the prospective resident wear and tear? Are elevators adequate? Do doors open in the right direction? Is the kitchen large enough to cook in for seven children and three adults? Are the bathrooms really safe for senior citizens? Can a bed be gotten around the corner and upstairs into the bedroom? Is there ample light and air, or does the fenestration cause more problems than it solves? These are just a few of the matters that must be carefully researched, analyzed, evaluated, and critiqued by the manager, and it must be done in light of past physical operating experience as well as the human response and reaction of those who will reside in the dwellings.

The manager must also prepare the management plan. This is the actual day-to-day handbook of operations that will ultimately serve to make the structure into a decent home. It is the bridge between the sponsor and the architect, and the building and the resident.

First, the general philosophy must be formulated, based upon the goals and objectives of the sponsors. This must be tempered and correlated to the actual design format and its practical and physical limitations. In brief, this is the beginning of the bridge building. One must always remain conscious of the objective of the program, the realities of the structure and the site, and the sensibilities of those who will use it in the years ahead.

THE OPERATING BUDGET

An operating budget must be devised that provides for the range of services—including social services—required by residents as well as for the short- and long-term requirements of the property. Staffing, rental collection, accounting, heating, painting, cleaning, maintenance, taxation, job descriptions, salary levels, social services—these are but a few of the many budget cost centers that must be planned for the day when the development becomes an actuality. The items of replacement reserve must be tabulated. Phasing of costs and activities must be carefully applied to the completion and occupancy of the living units.

The essential lifeblood of income must be calculated; this is a matter of social concern as well as practical application. With too little income the housing cannot be sustained over the long term—it will become depleted and depreciated long before it has fulfilled its expectations. The rents themselves must be applied and adjusted in light of those who will be served by this housing—their income levels, their pensions, their welfare income, or their life's capital, whatever it may be.

Now the harsh light of the early reality of determining the economic facts of life must be confronted—what is left over to pay for the debt that has been incurred in serving the public with decent housing? What are our financial commitments by the month and by the year? Can we meet these obligations now? Will we be able to meet them in the future? This is the real test of management planning—the area of expertise in which many of our current projects have fallen short.

Financial planning based upon real costs of operation and realistic rents is a function best filled by those in management who have taken part in the day-to-day struggle to operate the physical facilities in such a manner as to assure that it truly earns its income and sustains its value for future needs. The costs of operation are often neglected until the last minute. This is not to imply that someone does not do some fast calculations that are inaccurately labeled "operating costs." Experience has demonstrated that there is little reality to these mythical numbers so glibly articulated by those who have often planned or financed projects in the past.

Costs of operation are not just hastily arrived-at percentages; they represent complete and careful applications of knowledge correlated to the proposed structural program of utilization. Faulty operating budgets sow the seeds of project destruction, since inadequate operational procedures create a fertile field for resident lassitude in meeting their rental obligations. This begins the vicious circle of declining physical and social conditions that leads to decreased occupancy, increasing collection losses, and final destruction of the entire program so lovingly envisioned by the sponsor at its inception.

Thus, by creating a real management plan, with careful application costs and income, the management team assists in the realistic financing of the housing, since it cannot exist and cannot meet its objective of decent housing without paying its debts.

MANAGEMENT SENSITIVITY, RESPONSIVENESS,
AND PROFESSIONALISM

How does management gain sensitivity, responsiveness and professionalism? It all starts with people who are truly interested in other people. Property management is no place for those who cannot relate well to others. If one understands people, there is no more challenging a profession than property management.

Being a property manager is more than being a rent collector—the task that is so often confused with the other duties and obligations of the management team. It requires knowledge of how people can and will use a building for housing, for living, for loving, for playing, for being born, and for dying. The property manager must know accounting, bookkeeping, human motivation, personnel selection, maintenance, repairs, heating, landscaping, parking, and a whole encyclopedia of other operational tasks. The property manager does not have to be an expert in every detail, but he must have an appreciation and an understanding of all of the physical, financial, and human functions related to his particular property.

These functions must be learned and correlated; they must become second nature to the property manager. When these obligations are fully absorbed, they must be applied humanly and humanely to day-to-day operations.

Only when every daily task is properly done—for the residents, for the property, for the sponsor, and for the financial obligations—can management be said to be truly professional.

How does one learn all this? Obviously, the first step is practical experience coupled with continuing education. IREM has a fully accredited program for those operating at the property level called "The Accredited Resident Manager" (ARM). It consists of on-the-job training and a carefully detailed educational program covering the human, social, financial, and operational aspects of property management. The ARM program has been offered nationally since 1974 and is a valuable tool for advancement to professional ability and stature in property management. It fills a crying need for training for the thousands of people who must do the job if the promise of decent housing in the years ahead is to be kept—not only for the new developments to come, but to salvage those that have failed to meet reasonable expectations.

The ARM program is one of the levels of attainment that marks the professional. The institute offers further programs aimed at full certification in property management with the designation of CPM. Where the ARM program focuses upon the property and the people, the CPM programs move into the areas of property analysis, with intensive study of ownership objectives and capabilities, financing,

value, taxation, ownership forms, economic alternatives, deferred
maintenance, and curable obsolescense; all of these essential topics
are treated in terms of their impact upon the people who use the property and how decisions at the executive level will affect the lives and
activities of those for whom the housing has been designed.

This is the pathway to professionalism. When the management
team has earned its spurs, it can begin at the beginning by aiding in
every step of the way, from concept to objective and from design to
operation.

CONCLUSION

The management process helps keep the promise of decent housing when it knows and understands the human use of housing structures.
It must understand how people look at and use multifamily housing; it
will understand the budgeting process and the setting and attainment
of proper rental levels; it will recognize the obligation of mortgage
payments; it will prepare for the years ahead by understanding the
need for reserves for replacement. In short, management will operate the project so that it can and will do its intended job.

When that level of expertise is attained, it gains its own recognition as a full member in good standing of the planning and development team, giving management, operational, ownership, and resident
viewpoints so that a balanced plan is generated and executed that meets
and keeps the promise of decent housing. At that point, the housing
program can flourish in an atmosphere that allows for sensitivity to
grow and response to be recognized.

It starts with people who appreciate other people; people who
can understand property; managers who can analyze, plan, and exe-
cute and who do it with regard to the individuals who use the property
for which they are responsible. This is not to imply that he is a mere
do-gooder, because without operating knowledge and ability the best
of intentions soon prove ineffective. The property fails through ineptitude in meeting obligations to itself and to those it houses.

Sensitivity and responsiveness can only exist when there is a
plan. Response to expediency is not management at all—it is chaos.

The property manager must be knowledgeable and must be allowed, by fiat if necessary, to act in concert with all charged with
housing programs. Thankfully, the government has recognized this
need at last. By analysis, study, planning, and critique, the manager
works with others to produce livable housing that fulfills its aspirations.

Once again, one must know the cost, not just of the building and
the mortgage, but of the operations and attitudes and how these costs
serve those to whom we are dedicated. For if we do not know these

costs—all of them—we cannot build the structure; we cannot even lay a solid foundation.

1

ADVOCACY AND EDUCATION

THE CURRENT SITUATION

Housing is in crisis. At a time of growth in the total number of households caused by the coming of age of the children born in the baby boom after World War II, production is dropping and prices are rising.

Housing production is at its lowest level since World War II. Interest rates are at near-record levels. Many communities, concerned about the environmental impact of growth, are prohibiting or restricting production.

All of the traditional subsidy programs of HUD were frozen in January 1973. There remains only a trickle of production from projects approved prior to the freeze or those so far along in processing that HUD permitted them to continue.

The only active housing subsidy program through HUD is the Section 8 housing assistance payments program. This approach was embodied in the Housing and Community Development Act of 1974, which was approved in late August of that year. There are many serious reservations about the effectiveness and workability of Section 8. However, HUD is committed to making the program work, and appears to be open to criticisms and suggestions.

The basic problem with Section 8, viewed from the perspective of those concerned with giving the highest priority to those people with very low incomes and therefore the most critical housing needs, is that it is not designed to serve large numbers of low-income house-

---

The materials for the Action Guide were compiled and coordinated by Burke E. Dorworth.

holds. Moreover, tenant selection is in the hands of the developer, who can be expected to exclude very large families, families with children, or other families that are not easy to handle as tenants.

OPPORTUNITIES FOR ADVOCACY

The voices of those who are concerned with dealing with the housing crisis of low- and moderate-income families seem muted. Elected officials at all levels of government tend to feel that people who are interested in restricting growth, protecting the homogeneity of their neighborhoods, or avoiding the presence of large numbers of poor or minority people in their community are far stronger than those who wish to see effective measures taken to deal with our housing needs. Yet it should be clear that, without large-scale and costly housing subsidy programs, low-income people will continue to be inadequately housed.

Effective advocacy depends on an accurate knowledge of the needs of your own community and the ability to interpret and explain these needs to others. The following suggestions are designed with this in mind.

HOUSING NEEDS IN YOUR COMMUNITY

Most communities of 50,000 or more and many counties have, under the new Housing and Community Development Act, prepared Housing Assistance Plans. These plans are required for HUD funding of community development programs. They must identify the housing needs of all current community residents and of those who are employed in the community and may wish to reside there. Special attention must be given to the housing needs of the poor, moderate-income people, the elderly, large families, and minorities.

The Housing Assistance Plan is a public document and should be available from the local government. It is important as a first step to look at it and to ask whether the Housing Assistance Plan is a sound one. Does it accurately state the housing needs of the community? Does it provide housing not only for current residents but for others who may wish to reside in the community? Most important, how soon will the needs identified in the Housing Assistance Plan be met? Because of the extremely inadequate scale of housing subsidy programs, typically only a small fraction—perhaps 1 to 10 percent—of the housing needs of any community appear to be obtainable within a one- or two-year period.

In addition to examining the material in the Housing Assistance
Plan, there are several other critical questions that are relevant:
How many households in the community are paying more than 25 percent of their income for shelter? How many of these are low-income
families? How many people occupy housing units that are more than
30 years old and valued at less than $7,500 or renting for less than
$60? These questions are important because there are no good ways
of measuring inadequate housing using generally available census data.
The most usual criterion—housing that lacks plumbing facilities—is a
far more accurate indicator in rural areas than it is in cities, where
most units, however dilapidated, tend to have plumbing. However,
old housing units, unless they are subsidized, that are low in value or
in rent tend to be substandard. Thus, one can use the number of units
more than 30 years old and at the bottom end of the rent or value range
as an indicator of the number of housing units that probably need critical attention.

Resources for obtaining this information include the local and
regional planning commissions; the local housing authority, if there
is one; and the local agency that is charged with the administration of
housing and community development programs. In addition, two other
agencies that provide help in advocacy and education are the Citizen Advocate Center, 1145 19th Street, N.W., Washington, D.C. 20036,
and the National Peoples Action on Housing, 121 West Superior, Chi-
cao, Illinois 60610.

HOUSING SUBSIDIES IN YOUR COMMUNITY

Having identified the scale of housing needs, it is important to
see how well they are being met. To begin with, try to identify how
much subsidized housing there is and who lives in it. This means
how much public housing there is, including projects, large and small,
as well as scattered sites or released units; how much housing has
been provided through the below-market interest rate programs, such
as 235 and 236, and how much housing there is for the elderly. The
area office of HUD, which handles most of these subsidies, should be
able to provide this information, including breakdowns of the occupants by family size and income range.

It is more difficult to identify the indirect housing subsidies
through the tax system, although these will be much larger. As a
rough approximation, the 1970 census provides information on family
income. Take the number of families with incomes above $20,000
and multiply this by $500. This will give a low estimate of the tax
subsidies going into your community. (It is only an approximation
because these amounts vary according to the amount of interest de-

ducted and also according to the level of local property taxes. They
are based on national averages that show that more than 50 percent
of all households with incomes above $20,000 do take advantage of
such deductions and that the average value of the deduction at the
$20,000 level is $400.) It will be instructive to compare this annual
housing subsidy cost, provided as a matter of right by the federal
government, with the housing subsidies provided through HUD to the
directly subsidized projects.

COMMUNITY DEVELOPMENT PROGRAMS

If your community receives funding for community development,
obtain a copy of the plan and program and carefully review how adequately it covers housing needs; how full the provisions are for citizen participation; and, perhaps most important, whether there is continuing consideration of the use of community development funds to
meet housing needs.

Resources for this include the mayor's office, planning commission, and community development agency as well as the following national organizations, which have published useful materials describing
the community development program and how to monitor it: the Center
for Community Change, the National Association for the Advancement
of Colored People (NAACP), and the National Committee Against Discrimination in Housing.

SECTION 8 HOUSING ASSISTANCE PROGRAM

It is important to identify who is developing Section 8 housing
(this could be through a state agency program, through a local housing authority, or through private developers). It is particularly important to note whether Section 8 is operating through existing housing or whether new or substantially rehabilitated housing is being
provided, and who the occupants of Section 8 housing are. Compare
the information on what is happening with Section 8 with information
on housing needs. The best source of information on Section 8 will
probably be the area office of HUD.

GROWTH AND ACCESS TO LAND

Planning and zoning regulations often operate directly to either
restrict or limit growth or, perhaps even worse, to permit only the
development of expensive single-family houses serving the top 10,
15, or 20 percent of the income range. It is important to know

whether suitably located land is available for moderate-density housing, such as apartments or individually owned townhouses or condominiums. It is also important to know whether this land has public utilities available and, if not, what plans are being made to provide them. In communities with large minority populations, it is also important to note whether public services, such as water, sewers, and paved streets, are available in the minority sections and are of comparable quality to those in the remainder of the community. Resources for this information are primarily the local planning and zoning offices. It is also important to review the community's comprehensive plan to see what provision is being made for meeting the housing needs of low-income families that either reside in the community or are expected to do so.

CIVIL RIGHTS

Title 8 of the Civil Rights Act of 1968 prohibits discrimination in housing and gives HUD an affirmative duty to end the discriminatory dual housing market that is typical of communities with minority populations. HUD has issued advertising and affirmative marketing regulations that require all developers and real estate brokers to make housing available without discrimination and to advertise it in such a way that no racial bias is implied. The real estate advertising section of almost any local newspaper will contain violations of these guidelines and provisions. Moreover, except for fair-housing groups, which often function as service organizations, there has been little effective advocacy of the need to impose sanctions so that the legal requirements against discrimination are taken seriously. Resources for information on the local situation and needs for advocacy include fair-housing organizations and state and local human relations agencies, as well as branches of such national organizations as the NAACP and the National Urban League.

FEDERAL LEGISLATION

The adequacy of housing programs for low-income people depends almost entirely on the scale and scope of federal subsidy programs. It is important, therefore, to be in touch with what is happening in Congress. This should include not only proposals for substantive changes in federal programs but also the budget resolutions that Congress passes semiannually, which set the level of appropriations for housing and other activities, and the appropriations bills themselves. Housing is carried in two separate appropriations acts: the

HUD appropriations and the appropriations for the FmHA's rural programs, which are contained in the Agriculture appropriations bill. Resources for information on housing legislation include the Rural Housing Information Service, the National Rural Housing Coalition, the Ad Hoc Low Income Housing Coalition, the National Housing Conference, and the National Association of Home Builders.

STATE LEGISLATION

Increasingly, states are becoming involved in housing matters and are setting up state housing development corporations and state housing authorities. Information on this must obviously be obtained from state sources. In addition, the Council on State Governments, the Housing Assistance Council, the National Association of Housing and Redevelopment Officials, and some other national organizations do follow the major proposals that are being undertaken at the state level on a less systematic basis.

2

INTRODUCTION

This chapter is a guide to a nonprofit sponsor's process in housing low- and moderate-income families and senior citizens.

This is a guide. It is not meant to be a do-it-yourself kit. The emphasis is on the sponsor's engaging the best professional help available and working together with them in a relationship of trust.

With available programs and financing approaches in constant flux, this guide is an attempt to give a rather universal approach that should be able to provide guidance through any existing or future program. It is intended to make sponsors aware of the areas of decision; beyond that, specific needs and ingenuity will fill in the gaps as sponsors write their own action guides on the terrain of their community.

COMMUNICATING THE NEED

In the nonprofit housing development world, new or rehabilitated housing units come about because someone sees the need and becomes concerned enough to do something about it. To develop housing you must convince others until you have translated your personal concern into a highly motivated group concern. Developing housing is a long, tedious, exhausting, discouraging process. Follow-through is the essential ingredient. The key is commitment. That key turns the locks to open doors to new housing units for families and senior citizens who won't get there without you. When you see that happen once, the exhilaration will start you on the process all over again.

Whatever turned you on to the housing need—whether it was seeing the substandard housing where you live, reading newspaper articles or viewing a television report, or some chance remark by someone looking for decent housing—someone or some experience has given you new eyesight, and things that you may have previously passed by without a glance now absorb you. You know that the need for family and senior citizen housing in your community is real. Now you want to translate that knowledge into brick and mortar. You are ready to persuade others to be a part of a committed solution.

At this stage, it is not too early to seek help from housing offices. Presumably, you are part of a group whose leaders you will approach to become the support base for the development work ahead. Find out from your leaders what regional or national office of your group has responsibility in the housing field. Discuss with that office what you have seen and what you propose to do about it. Learn what assistance is available—technical, financial, or moral. Beyond this, you will most likely be on your own and it will be you who will muster the support to move ahead.

Often, patience is required to bring others around. Perhaps a windshield tour of areas where housing is obviously deteriorated would help. Get others to talk with people who need better housing; confer with social workers, health and welfare offices, plant managers, housing agencies, senior citizen groups, and people who know the conditions. Your determination will convince enough members of your parent group whose sensitivities, like your own, will bring a strong resolve to be a part of the solution. With that support, you are ready to begin on a serious scale.

OBTAINING PARENT-BODY APPROVAL

A few committed people will need to determine what is wanted before the parent body is asked for formal endorsement. This stage would be a good time to hold a session at which a housing consultant sketches the process. Perhaps your group office will supply such an expert to orient your group in these early stages. Or you may be referred to a housing consultant who will "brainstorm" with you. This person can guide you in the initial phase so that you will be able to answer the following questions:

1. What kind of housing do you want to develop?
2. What federal, state, or conventional housing programs are available?
3. How do you arrange for a suitable development site?
4. How would the project be financed?
5. What professionals will be part of the development team?
6. What financial expectations and risks are involved?
7. How do you organize for development?

This meeting should also set the plans for a similar, but carefully planned, presentation to your parent body so that its sponsorship
approval will be obtained. The reason for this is that, whether you
utilize a federal insuring program, a state-financed program, or a
bond or conventionally financed program or enter into a limited partnership agreement, those capable of providing the financing will want
to be working with a viable nonprofit sponsor.

To determine whether an organization is an eligible nonprofit
sponsor, the following questions, in one form or another, must be
asked:

1. How long has the nonprofit organization been in existence?
The length of time in a community is important to any lender who
wants to be assured that an organization is likely to be in existence
for the life of the project mortgage. Since that mortgage could be
anywhere from 35 to 55 years, if it can show that it has already been
in existence that long, it will be considered likely to exist that many
more years into the future.

2. What is the organization's history of social service and
charity to the community? Special committees that show a community
concern are important bench marks of an organization's sincerity of
purpose.

3. What are the motivations of the organization in developing
housing? Past service to the community can show the consistency of
objective in housing sponsorship. The organization will be able to
show that it is seeking to develop a housing project out of its own desire to provide decent housing and is not serving as a front organization for some distant developer.

4. What support does the organization have in the development
of the housing project? The financial picture of the parent organization will show a fiscal base that indicates sound financing judgment
is a part of its history. Beyond this, the past and present leadership
reputation of the organization can be a factor in determining the kind
of leadership capabilities that will be present in the housing corporation.

5. Is the size of the organization consistent with the responsi-
bilities and size of the proposed project? An organization of 30 members might be considered a doubtful developer of a 200-unit senior
citizen project. There are no hard and fast rules here; common
sense will indicate a project size commensurate with organizational
strength.

These tests of sponsorship eligibility provide the rationale for
seeking broader support. Now, with your leaders, check the consti-
tutional requirements of your organizational body as to how your new

housing corporation can be established with proper credentials. For
example, the Baptist Conventions require a majority vote of a con-
gregational meeting to establish support of a separate corporation under that church's auspices. The Presbyterian Church requires a
favorable vote of its governing body, the session, for such support.

Whatever is required, do not move ahead of your support. Do
not make any commitments without gaining the proper support. Plan
at this stage to prepare adequate information to make your presentation to the proper parent body, realizing that you will want a resolution passed along the lines of the one presented in Figure 5.

What will it take to get this kind of a resolution passed by the
proper authority of your group? Some groups have persuaded their
parent bodies by preparing brief but comprehensive papers outlining
such matters as the work of a task force on housing and the facts of
its community's housing as discovered by that task force; the rationale
for decent housing for all citizens (see the preceding chapter on Advocacy and Education); the history of nonprofit organizations in meeting
housing needs; a description of the housing project envisioned by the
task force; an accounting of how other community agencies describe
the local housing need; a listing of programs available to finance the
development; an outline of the development phases; and a description
of available professional assistance.

Such exhibits are meant to assure those who have not experienced
what you have that you know what you are talking about, that the need
is real, that development programs are available, and that it is a
reasonable request to ask for authority to incorporate as a nonprofit
developer of housing under the auspices of the parent body.

HOW MUCH WILL IT COST?

When you are satisfied that you can present a clear picture of
the problem and how you can be a part of its solution if given the proper
backing, you are ready to make your presentation, except on one
count. How much will it cost?

Once upon a time one could confidently say that a good nonprofit
housing developer should be able to build housing without putting up
any money. Everyone worked on a contingency basis unless money
were available in front-money loans from the government or an agency
Today this is not as likely to be the situation. Money will be required.
In the period before financing is secured and the project goes into
construction, it is reasonable to anticipate that about $30,000 will
be needed by the sponsor for items such as site control option; attorney fees for organizational fees; rezoning, if required; consultant
fees for guiding the development team, for economic feasibility

FIGURE 5

Institutions Resolution to Sponsor Housing

WHEREAS, the membership of _____ is aware of the severe shortage of safe, decent, and sanitary housing for people of low and moderate incomes within the _____ area; and

WHEREAS, man's need for safe, decent, and sanitary housing within his financial means has long been a concern of this organization, and continues to be a concern of its members; and

WHEREAS, certain sections of the National Housing Act and/or the state's financing agency and other conventional programs provide opportunities for nonprofit organizations to participate in the provision of housing for low- and moderate-income families by sponsoring housing developments; and

WHEREAS, the sponsorship of such a housing development is in keeping with the general purposes of this organization; and

WHEREAS, we recognize our moral responsibility to sustain any housing project developed through the sponsoring corporation for which we have appointed representatives;

NOW, THEREFORE, BE IT RESOLVED that the members of _____ _____ do authorize and permit the following:

    (1) The sponsorship, alone or together with one or more other organizations with similar goals, of a low/moderate-income housing development financed with available mortgage funds

    (2) The formation, alone or together with one or more other organizations with similar goals, of a nonprofit mortgagor corporation under the permanent control of the sponsors to build and/or rehabilitate housing for rental and/or sale to persons of low/moderate incomes

    (3) The provision, in the case of housing developed for rental, of continuing and competent management for the project, and, in the case of housing developed for sale, of continuing budget and credit counseling to those homebuyers who need such counseling

    (4) To endeavor to provide financial support for the initiation of the development and, if it should become necessary, the assistance in further financial support for its continued operation on a long-term basis, recognizing this is a moral, and not a legal, obligation on our part

This the _____ day of _____, 19___.

                    BY:_____

                    TITLE:_____

I, _____, do hereby certify that I am the Secretary of _____, and that the foregoing is a true and correct copy of a resolution duly adopted by members of said organization at a meeting duly called on the _____ day of _____, 19___, after proper notice, and at which time a quorum was present, and as same appears on the books and records of said organization.

                                _____
                                        Secretary

studies, and for application development; and architectural fees for the preliminary drawings.

Engineering and application fees are returnable at initial closing (start of construction) from interim or construction financing and eventually become a part of the mortgage. The fact that up to $30,000 might become the initial responsibility of the nonprofit sponsor need not be a deterrent to moving ahead. It needs to be viewed realistically and advice must be sought on how it might be made available. Go over this situation with a consultant, who might suggest the following possibilities:

1. A loan from the parent body at the local or national level,

2. Loans from individuals concerned about community housing,

3. A loan from a government agency at the local, regional, or national level (the Appalachian Regional Commission makes such loans to nonprofit sponsors for many housing programs in its 13-state region),

4. A loan from a member of the development team, such as the general contractor,

5. Involvement in a limited partnership in which investors would handle all front-money and equity requirements,

6. A bond financing program in which monies are raised for the entire project development costs on a planned pay-back basis.

One very successful nonprofit developer, Improved Dwellings for Altoona (IDA) (Pennsylvania), has served its community as a broadly based ecumenical corporation composed of Catholic, Protestant, and Jewish organizations. In the late 1960s, each religious group placed an amount of money into the total fund until there was nearly $40,000 to be used by the corporation to develop housing. They used that money on a revolving-fund basis and have developed nearly 200 units of new family and senior citizen housing as a nonprofit sponsor and in a limited partnership arrangement. In addition, IDA has rehabilitated other units in the city. There are other, similar examples. The need of cash requirements is just one more problem that is within your grasp to solve.

Now that you feel confident that all questions can be answered to the satisfaction of the general audience, you are ready to ask your parent body to pass the housing resolution. Set the meeting date. Encourage those sensitive to your purposes to be present. Request a consultant whom you anticipate contracting with to be present at the meeting to field technical questions regarding programs and financing.

THE ORGANIZING COMMITTEE

If all goes well, the parent body is now on record as the sponsor and has appointed the recommended persons to serve as an organizing committee for the mortgagor corporation—the actual working group that will develop the project.

To reach this meeting, a great deal has already been accomplished. Step by logical step, you have reached the stage at which the actual planning of a housing project can begin. A few items are required to secure this base:

1. Draw up a list of organizing committee members with their full addresses and telephone numbers.

2. Elect interim officers whom you anticipate will be your first full-time officers elected following incorporation: president, vice president, secretary, and treasurer.

3. If your group has too many members to allow it to act decisively, elect an executive committee represented by all groups with the power to act. Such a committee might range in size from nine to fifteen members.

4. Form initial committees, such as an organizational committee charged with arranging for articles of incorporation and bylaws, a finance committee charged with fund-raising recommendations, and a site committee charged with locating possible sites suitable for the project that has been decided upon.

5. Determine a bank at which the treasurer will establish the corporation's account, and direct the treasurer to keep complete records. Financial statements will be required.

6. Instruct the secretary to keep formal records of all meeting proceedings and to be aware that such records may prove helpful in establishing the eligibility of the corporation as a viable nonprofit sponsor. The secretary should also be instructed to sent out notices of all future meetings.

7. Select a consultant and request that a memorandum of agreement be submitted so that a formal contract can be entered into.

THE CONSULTANT

Since the consultant should guide and counsel the nonprofit sponsor in all phases of organization, including the selection of the development team, economic studies, and development, he should perform the following services:

1. Assist the sponsor in selecting and establishing contracts with all members of the development team: the attorney, the economist (market analysis), the architect, the general contractor, the mortgagee, the realtor, and the management.

2. Assist the individuals of the development team with information pertinent to the sponsor's organizational and developmental tasks as related to the government insuring and financing agencies familiar to the consultant.

3. Assist in making an economic feasibility study of pertinent market data to determine the type of housing suitable for the sponsor's purposes and for the neighborhood or area in which the project would be located, the number of units suitable and appropriate to applicable zoning, the approximate rentals to be charged, and a general analysis of all information required for a professional development of the project.

4. Assist in selecting a suitable site for the project's location and, if necessary, aid in obtaining appraisals of land and arranging suitable terms for the purchase of real property or, if required, obtaining a long-term lease acceptable to financing agencies.

5. Assist in the preparation of all applications and exhibits required for financing and aid the sponsor in obtaining the best possible construction and permanent mortgage loans.

6. Assist in obtaining the required front-money financing from sources available for that purpose. Compensation for the consultant is often 1 percent of the mortgage amount, although usually no less than $15,000 and no more than $25,000 with a willingness to accept whatever lesser amount a government insuring or financing agency would establish. This amount is typically paid on the basis of 75 percent at initial closing (start of construction) and 25 percent at final closing. When retainers are established, as is more often the situation today, a typical arrangement is to pay the consultant a $500 monthly retainer for 12 months. If the project has not gone to initial closing by that time, the consultant works without additional compensation until it closes. All monies advanced by retainer are reimbursed to the sponsor at closing from fees permitted at that time.

THE ATTORNEY

The consultant will aid in the selection of an attorney who understands your special needs and limited financing capabilities. If the attorney is to serve as the closing as well as the incorporating attorney, he should be experienced with the required federal or state forms and procedures. The fee schedule of the attorney is negotiable and should be clearly understood before formal arrangements for services are concluded. The Pennsylvania Housing Finance Agency allows a set amount for legal fees within the mortgage and suggests that such fees cover the following:

> 1) organizing the mortgagor entity and qualifying it under relevant housing and tax provisions of federal, state and local law; 2) obtaining legal control of or title to the building site; 3) preparation of required closing and construction documents, and supervision of their execution and 4) providing general counsel, as needed, together with all other reasonable and necessary legal services, excluding litigation, to enable the development to successfully achieve closing, construction, completion and occupancy.

The attorney's first duty is, with your assistance, to incorporate your organization under the laws of your state. Your organizing committee should provide the attorney with the desired name of the corporation and the names of the required number of incorportors.

Within this time frame, the attorney should also apply for a 501(c)(3) status as a charitable organization with the Office of Internal Revenue in order to permit tax deductible, charitable contributions to be made to the corporation. The 501(c)(3) status has become increasingly difficult to obtain. Service to the community as a nonprofit housing developer is not in itself sufficient justification for such status. A history of your parent body's charitable contributions of various services to the community and a listing of your own projected charitable services will help you to better make your case.

The attorney can also be helpful at this stage in establishing bylaws for the corporation's operation. These will also be required as exhibits for financing purposes.

THE HOUSING MARKET ANALYSIS

At this organizational stage, a number of matters can be handled concurrently: market analysis, site selection, and the engaging of a development team.

You know approximately what housing market you wish to serve: family, senior citizen, nursing home, and so on. You may have to be more certain that a market exists in sufficient quantity to justify your efforts. It will then be necessary to engage an economist skilled in conducting market analyses. Depending upon the scope of the study, the cost will range from a few thousand to ten thousand dollars or more.

A housing market analysis should be the first step taken by the prospective sponsors in housing development. Not only is such an analysis instrumental in guiding the developer/sponsor into sound development programs, but public financing and assistance sources and private lenders require market analysis as a preface to their consideration of support for a proposed project.

Market analysis provides guidance on current market conditions and the prospective quantitative and qualitative demand for additional housing, the impact of expanded or curtailed economic activity on the demand for housing, and the degree to which a proposed project will meet these identified demands. In addition, with the introduction of various forms of housing assistance over the last decade and a half, identification of housing need as distinguished from housing demand has become significant. Because the assistance programs reduce costs to users substantially below market rates, the concept of effective, or income-qualified, demand is less controlling.

Frequently, housing developments succeed or fail on the basis of qualitative factors, such as bedroom mix, size of units, and housing amenities. Accordingly, a principal purpose of the housing market analysis is to assure that the development is properly designed to serve the market it is intended to serve.

Housing market analysis may be described as a process of determining present and prospective housing demand/supply relationships in a local housing market. It encompasses a broad-scale analysis of forces affecting economic, demographic, and housing conditions and inventory trends. It includes the collection, analysis, and interpretation of data and subsequent presentation in a documented report of findings concerning past and prospective economic, population, and housing conditions and trends in the local market. It requires current estimates of employment, family incomes, population, households, residential construction, and vacancies as well as the projection of these basic factors. In addition to local factors, external influences—state, regional, and national—also affect economics and demand.

Thus, in broad terms, housing market analysis is concerned with the following:

1. Delineation of the market area—that is, the area within which dwelling units are competitive with one another;

2. The area's economy—principal economic activities, basic resources, and economic trends;

3. Demand factors, such as employment, incomes, population, households, and family size;

4. Supply factors, such as residential construction activity, housing inventory, conversions, and demolitions;

5. Current market conditions, including vacancies, unsold inventory, market ability of sales and rental units, prices, rents, and building costs;

6. Quantitative and qualitative demand—that is, the prospective number of dwelling units that can be absorbed economically at various price and rent levels.

There is no single sanctioned method of approach in conducting housing market analyses. Rather, there are a number of factors that must be considered and analyzed. The depth of analysis of each of the factors will depend upon the individual market of project situation and, to some degree, the individual judgment of the analyst.

In all instances of market analysis, the definition of the geographic area to be examined is mandatory. The traditional view of the housing market involves the idea of competitive interchangeability. Thus, the geographic housing market is that area in which all of the dwelling units are reasonably in competition with one another. Understandably, there are various market segments within the overall market, such as by tenure and by income/cost, which tend to transcend the principle of pure substitutability throughout the market. Nevertheless, the geographic scope of the market should reflect these considerations. The lack of precision as to exact market area boundaries is compounded by the limitations of available data. Typically, an accommodation is effected in determining a set of boundaries that will constitute the most reasonable and useful market area from the standpoint of the availability of data consistent with the analytical requirements. This plus firsthand observation throughout the area enables the analyst to substantially comply with the criterion of dwelling unit competition in delineating the housing market area.

During this stage of the analysis, consideration is given to transportation facilities, principal locations of employment, local commuting habits and preferences, developments, and topography. Observations and map study provide the analyst with the required perspective on the extent and structure of urban development, its direction of growth, and the pattern of major residential sectors.

Within a housing market area, dwelling units are linked in various patterns relative to individual preferences as to the type, quality, location, and so on of the dwelling unit desired. The housing market analysis will determine the appropriate submarket segmentation. These submarkets are distinguished by specific characteristics, such as tenure (sales and rental housing), price, rent, size in terms of bedrooms, height, special purpose (such as elderly or military), and location. Many more segmentations are conceivable, but these are the most commonly used in current market analysis practice.

The analysis of local housing market conditions and prospective demand for additional housing is dependent on an analysis of the economy of the market area. The economy of the area is analyzed with the objective of projecting economic outlook in terms of employment and other factors. Employment opportunities constitute the principal determinant of population growth; population is translated into households; and households are the units of demand for housing. There are, of course, exceptions to the primacy of employment base analysis, such as housing for the elderly. However, even in these instances it is still well for the analyst to become familiar with employment trends in the housing market area. In the long run, these trends will control the dynamics of housing supply and demand and thus influence the potential availability of housing for special groups such as the elderly.

The analytical approach to the economy of the market area is basically the same type of analysis. Scope, depth, and refinement may vary, depending upon the specific purpose, the cost in relation to the available budget, and the time schedule requirement. Variations in the types of analysis range from a relatively simple survey of business conditions and trends revealed by readily available statistics to an intensive analysis of a community's economic support. Typically, the following methodological steps are undertaken: review and evaluation is made of secondary published data related to the housing market area. This data is utilized in establishing the major economic trends that might have a bearing on the development of housing in the housing in the housing market. Factors usually considered include employment trends, population growth trends and characteristics, demographic characteristics (age, income, sex, and so on), immigration patterns, and other statistical material that is deemed pertinent.

In accomplishing this task, the analyst relies on data from the federal and state departments of labor and industry or employment commissions to analyze the economic base of the housing market. This analysis includes, in particular, identification and expected impact on job opportunities of new industry locations (or, conversely, plant closings). Since many housing markets rely partially on military connected residents, the analyst assesses the outlook for housing demand as induced from military facilities, where appropriate.

Particular emphasis is placed on projection of family income levels. To the degree that income levels continue to lag behind cost levels, there is increasing demand for various forms of housing assistance. The income analysis also provides important insight into future trends in tenure and unit-size considerations.

A major element in the analysis is examination of existing housing conditions in the housing market area. Typically, data on housing types, size, conditions, tenure, occupancy, and so on are drawn from the most recent U.S. Census of Housing, local area reports on building permits and demolitions, and other current market data. Comparable data from earlier U.S. censuses is tabulated and an analysis is made of trends or changes found in type, size, age, condition, price or rent, tenure, occupancy, and so on.

This task usually includes a close analysis of standard versus substandard units in the housing market, since, during periods of modest population growth, the replacement of deficient housing becomes relatively more significant. Also, it is usually the very sectors of the local society, such as the old and the poor, that occupy deficient housing and that are most in need of new units.

Frequently, an analysis is made of the development of residential areas of the housing market area, including the location, type, and number of units in publicly owned or publicly aided housing developments.

The most effective means of establishing what the existing housing conditions in the housing market are is through field identification of competitive developments and description of their characteristics and physical design. Identification and comparison is then made with the proposed development in terms of amenities offered, specific rent schedules (both current and projected), utility charges, vacancy rates, tenant profiles, turnover rates, marketing inducements, and rent-up periods. Typically, this task represents an in-depth field survey of major sales and rental apartment developments in the housing market.

Factors usually analyzed include physical characteristics, such as location, project size, parking, furnishings, design features, amenities, appearance, and evaluation; unit description, including price and rental levels and current occupancy and vacancy; market type and competitiveness to the project under study; owner and tenant characteristics, including place of employment, family size, and so on; and other survey factors deemed pertinent.

If a specific site for new housing within the housing market is under control or under consideration, the analyst evaluates the site in terms of a number of factors. Again, these factors vary according to the project under study and the market. However, typically included are delineation and analysis of available community and commercial facilities, including schools, shopping, transportation, health, and recreation; vacancy rates in the immediate area (from a comparable survey); nearby present and proposed land uses; zoning requirements; analysis of the site in terms of access and site configuration; identification and assessment of the impact of public plans and programs, such as urban renewal, transportation, and health and education, as well as other potential or planned land developments; identification of the availability and cost of the installation of utilities; and review and analysis of environmental factors, including site and area characteristics that would affect development or that should be taken into account in designing the development for the site.

Based upon the methods of approach outlined here, the analyst is now prepared to develop conclusions and recommendations related to the establishment of economic trends in the housing market and the ramifications of such trends for housing development; estimates of the future number of households compared with the existing housing stock to establish the range of demand for additional housing; the analysis of the present distribution of households to determine trends in the demand for dwelling units of different sizes and types; the projection of income levels to determine demand for dwelling units at different price and rent levels (comparison is made with the existing inventory of units to determine possible market shortages or surpluses); and, based upon the above, projected demand for residential units by type in the housing market for 15 to 20 years in five-year increments.

Following the identification of basic market data as described above, the analyst can use this data to arrive at pertinent recommendations with regard to possible development of new housing in the housing market. Typically, recommendations include the mix of residential markets offering the greatest demand in the housing market; evaluation of the potential site with regard to surrounding land uses and proposed future uses, circulation and access, proximity to shopping, transportation, other residential development, health, and social services, and other physical factors deemed pertinent; project development factors such as the optimum mix of housing types, including conventionally financed and publicly assisted, the established absorption rate for the proposed housing mix concept, taking into account the availability of comparable housing and the demand potential developed in the housing market analysis, and the consideration of income factors, particularly with regard to assistance housing programs and their impact on unit absorption; the formulation of a development approach, containing counsel on matters such as the type of unit in demand, the size of the unit in demand, the unit mixes most appropriate to the market, the unit price rental schedules, housing amenities, and the timing and phasing of development.

The housing market analysis and the analyst who performs it are critical elements and participants in the housing development process. Assuming he is called upon early enough in the process, the housing market analyst can guide the development toward the most productive and serviceable housing concepts. Accordingly, these can be carried out with a minimum of delay and confusion and with an optimum opportunity to attract sufficient financing and government support assistance.

SITE SELECTION

The following are some of the factors to be considered in making a site search:

1. Compare the requirements of size to the projected size and type of housing units. One rule of thumb is that 10 townhouses, 20 garden-type apartments (unit over a unit in a two-story walkup), or at least 40 high-rise units can normally be built on an acre of ground.

2. Check for availability of water, sewers, storm drainage, and an acceptable paved access to the site. If these items require off-site construction, the cost is normally excluded in government-insured or financed mortgage costs and either are covered by the land purchase price or must be borne by the developer.

3. Zoning must be adequate to handle the density and type of structure you propose. Any option agreement should be contingent upon proper zoning being obtained. You will have the financial responsibility for any rezoning effort required and you should seek proper legal advice concerning rezoning requirements and the atmosphere present for such efforts.

4. The topography of the site will have a direct bearing on how it might be developed. Your consultant and an architect will point out the advantages and disadvantages of the terrain.

5. How does the surrounding neighborhood match the units you propose? What is the character of the neighborhood?

6. What is the proximity of the site to such amenities as schools, shopping, transportation, churches, and recreation?

7. Is the cost of the site commensurate with your housing plans? Government insuring and financing agencies will only permit a certain amount of the mortgage money to be spent on the site. Usually such amounts are determined on a unit land cost, that is, for every new unit to be built on the site, what is its proportionate share of the land cost? Divide total land cost by the number of units planned to find the unit land cost.

8. Can the owner provide clear title to the site? Any cloud on the title would make it prohibitive as a site for financing.

9. Will the site pass the environmental impact criteria of your area?

THE PROFESSIONAL REAL ESTATE AGENT

It is widely believed that a nonprofit organization can save money by purchasing land suitable for a subsidized housing project directly from the owner. This direct purchase avoids a real estate commission, to be sure, and, so it is thought, the per-unit cost for the site will thereby be significantly reduced.

While such may be the case in some instances, it is perhaps more frequently true that an experienced real estate agent can secure the land at a lower per-unit cost, even with his commission included, than the nonprofit organization could have bought it for, operating without the agent's services.

This economy in the purchase of land may be realized by the purchaser's becoming the client of the agent. This relationship is permitted by the laws governing the licensing of real estate agents and is so natural a relationship that it is strange that so many people are surprised by the idea.

Typically, the real estate agent works for, and in the best interests of, the property owner, simply because the property owner has agreed to pay the agent a commission for bringing him an acceptable contract. The property owner is thus the real estate agent's client for whoever pays, or agrees to pay, the agent's commission is, strictly speaking, the client. The agent is, therefore, under a fiduciary obligation to bring the owner—his client—the best price and terms possible for the property being offered for sale.

Having established this relationship, the agent cannot ethically work in the best interests of the prospective buyer. On the contrary, he must strive to secure the best price and the best possible terms for the land for the property owner in order to be faithful to the fiduciary responsibility he has assumed.

If the agent suggests to the prospective buyer that, in his opinion, the property is overpriced and can be obtained for less, he has violated the Code of Ethics of the National Association of Realtors, because he is guilty of a conflict of interest.

Typically, the agent works for the property owner, but there is no reason why he cannot work for the prospective buyer if the buyer will agree to become the client; that is, if the buyer will agree to pay the agent's commission. With this change in the client-agent relationship, the agent's fiduciary responsibility is transferred to the buyer. He no longer is working for, and in behalf of, the seller.

When the buyer becomes the client, the agent is freed from the customary restraints that govern his behavior when he is working as the agent for the property owner. He can now freely advise his client —the buyer—on the market value of the various properties available for purchase. He can make recommendations regarding the price and terms to offer a seller, and, perhaps most important of all, he can approach the seller in a new way. By putting the seller and any other real estate agents who may be involved on notice that his commission is being paid by the purchaser, he is free to negotiate the lowest possible price and the best possible terms for his client, the purchaser.

This kind of approach frequently results in a purchase price that is well below the market price on the property, even with the payment of the normal real estate commission to the agent.

There are, of course, other reasons for employing the services of a professional real estate agent besides seeking to secure a more favorable price. The agent can save the nonprofit organization considerable time by researching and selecting land that has the appropriate zoning. Rezoning has become such a time-consuming process in most major metropolitan areas that much time is lost by the uninitiated in looking at land that probably is unsuitable or for which zoning cannot be obtained or cannot be obtained within the time frame required.

Furthermore, the agent will draw up a contract in such a way that the land is sufficiently under the control of the purchaser to allow him to proceed to seek financing. At the same time, he will ensure that the kinds of contingency are included in the contract that will safeguard the nonprofit organization against liability in case the project is infeasible for any reason.

Real estate agents with proper professional credentials and experience in commercial real estate are available in most areas in which nonprofit organizations would be engaged in housing projects. Consult your local board of realtors for recommendations regarding qualified commercial real estate agents and select the one you feel will give you the best service.

Once the site has been selected, your attorney will know the local situation and assist you with an option to cover local rules and regulations and customs.

THE DEVELOPMENT TEAM

Not all members of the development team are required at the same time. Some guidelines for the engagement of each member are presented here in the form of questions you might put to each.

The Architect

1. Is the architect willing to work within the framework of front monies secured without additional expense to the nonprofit sponsor if the project does not go through?

2. As an architect, is he willing to design within the budget established by a letter of feasibility?

3. Is he willing to accept design limitations established by the insuring or financing agency?

4. Is he willing to modify his plans after completion if they do not meet the cost limits—and at no additional expense to the sponsor?

5. Would he be willing to work with the sponsor and consultant to work out difficulties that might arise with the government agencies involved?

6. If it is a HUD-insured project, does he understand the working relationship established with HUD's design representative?

7. Is he willing to meet the time deadlines imposed by the insuring or finance agency?

8. Is he willing to assist the builder in costing out the project?

9. Has he already accomplished a HUD project?

10. Has he worked with the local insuring office?

11. How many staff members are in his offices, as an indication of his capability to handle multifamily projects?

After these questions have been answered to your satisfaction, you should be able to conclude that the architect understands the limitations of budget and design imposed by the agencies involved and that he has a social concern for the people you intend to serve.

The General Contractor

1. Is the general contractor willing to sign an incentive contract with the sponsor, based upon the construction amount set by the insurir or financing agency?

2. Does he understand that he is bound to pay prevailing wages as established for the area if it is a HUD-insured project?

3. Does he know that he is to cost certify construction costs and fees paid to the satisfaction of HUD?

4. Will he be able to obtain adequate bond?

5. Is he willing to assist the architect to bring the project within the allowable budget?

6. Does he accept the responsibility to construct within the time limit established?

7. Will he begin construction within 12 days following initial closing, whenever that should take place?

8. Does he understand HUD inspection procedures and that there will be architectural supervision during construction by the design architect or an architect designated by the sponsor?

9. Will he assist the sponsor with the timely completion of all exhibits assigned to him so that the sponsor will be able to meet the established schedule to make application for firm commitment?

10. Does he understand his obligation to Equal Employment Opportunity Certification?

11. Does he accept the fact that his overhead and profit amounts are established by HUD?

12. Is he willing to accept the land development and structure cost as established by FHA ?

13. Has he ever constructed a HUD project before ?

14. Has he worked with the local insuring office of HUD before?

15. What experience leads him to conclude that he can construct this project ?

After these questions have been answered to your satisfaction, you should be able to conclude that the general contractor understands the limitations of your budget; he accepts the responsibility to work closely with the architects during the design phase in order to effect the most economically designed project; he is capable of constructing the job under FHA specifications and within the allowable time period; he is likely to be acceptable to the insuring or financing agency; and he will cooperate with the sponsor in the preparation of required exhibits necessary to take the project to firm application.

The Managing Agent

In recognition of the ratio between defaults and bad management, the insuring and financing agencies have initiated stricter guidelines and controls on managing agents. Your questions to prospective management should reflect this concern.

1. How many projects of the nature of your proposed development has he managed?

2. What is the nature of the accounting system, rent-up procedure, rent collection policy, and preventive maintenance program he would use with the proposed project?

3. How would he utilize available community services for tenants ?

4. What is his approach to tenant organizations ?

5. What are his expectations of the sponsor in the management relationship?

6. What is his method of supervision of the resident manager ?

7. How does he handle tenant grievances and what counseling services to tenants does he provide ?

8. What training programs does he have for tenants and for the resident manager ?

9. Has he developed a management plan suitable for government approval?

10. Has he worked with the affirmative marketing plan?

11. What is his overall philosophy of management ?

12. What is the size of his organization, as an indication of capability for managing the project ?

After these questions have been answered to your satisfaction, you should be able to conclude that the management will be sensitive to the special needs of your tenants and will conduct its affairs in a thorough, businesslike manner.

THE ECONOMIC FEASIBILITY STUDY

Utilizing the expertise and educated guesses of the development team, the consultant will take the numbers accumulated up to this point and provide a preliminary feasibility study based on the best financing program available for the housing you wish to develop. The mortgage amount will be based on the following items:

1. The builder's costs, including the structure (materials and labor), land improvement, general requirements, overhead, profit, bond premium, and off-site improvements;

2. Architectural fees for the design of the building, engineering costs, and supervision of construction;

3. Financing costs, including the cost of borrowing money for the construction phase, based on current interest rates, application fees, title and recording fees; insurance fees during construction; taxes during construction; permanent financing standby fees; and servicing fees;

4. Miscellaneous fees, including the attorney's fee and legal expenses, organizational fees, the consultant's fee, the contingency reserve, and the cost of the land.

The total of these costs will give you the estimated replacement cost. Depending upon the current debt service factor and the years the mortgage will run, the estimated replacement cost will lead to a determination of the amount of net income required annually to pay the mortgage. To this amount must be added the annual operating expenses, as follows:

1. Management costs, including profit and advertising;

2. Operating costs, such as elevator maintenance, utilities, trash removal, and payroll;

3. Maintenance costs, such as decorating, repairs, exterminating, insurance, ground expense, and the replacement reserve;

4. Taxes, including real estate, property, and payroll taxes.

The total of these costs will give you the annual operating expenses. Now total these expenses and the required net income to amoratize the mortgage. Assume a 93 to 95 percent occupancy of the final structure, and rents for individual units can be determined.

Your consultant will work with the numbers given him for these
various items and determine if they lead to an economically feasible
project with rents commensurate with the needs of the people you wish
to serve. Once these numbers are right, regardless of the program
you utilize or the financing route to be followed, the application process can begin.

SECTIONS 8 AND 202 PROGRAMS

Since January 1973, when housing development programs popular
with nonprofit developers were placed in moratorium, there have been
few alternatives for developing decent housing for low- and moderate-
income persons. The preceding chapter on Advocacy and Education
discussed continuous attempts to revive those programs through legislative action. You may want to be a part of this effort to reinitiate
programs in which the federal government subsidizes the permanent
financing interest rate down to 1 percent, which has the effect of reducing the rent by about one-third of the required market rent to amoratize the project mortgage.

In the meantime, there is currently one federal program that
provides rent assistance and can be applied whether you finance under
an acceptable HUD-insured program, a State Housing Finance Agency
direct-loan program, or other financing arrangements acceptable to
HUD. This program is the Section 8 Leased Housing Program. The
information provided here is from a HUD "Fact Sheet" and from an in-
formative question-answer paper developed by the National Housing
Partnerships. This is followed by a brief explanation of the Section
202 housing program for the elderly.

Section 8 Housing Assistance Payments Program

The Section 8 Housing Assistance Payments Program was authorized by the Housing Act of 1937 as amended by Section 201 of the Housing and Community Development Act of 1974.

Its basic concept is that HUD will provide housing assistance
payments on behalf of eligible lower-income families (families whose
income does not exceed 80 percent of the median income for the locality) occupying newly constructed, substantially rehabilitated, or existing housing. This payment will make up the difference between the
approved rent for the unit and the amount the family is required to
pay, which will be not less than 15 percent and not more than 25 percent of the family's adjusted income.

Participating housing projects may be owned by private owners,
both for-profit and nonprofit, or by public housing agencies. To par-

ticipate, owners will submit development proposals in response to a
HUD-published invitation for proposals. If both the preliminary and
final proposals are acceptable to HUD, HUD will enter into an agreement that, upon completion of the project, it will enter into a Housing
Assistance Payments Contract with the owner for a specified term.
Under this contract, HUD will make housing assistance payments with
respect to units occupied by eligible families.

Any type of financing may be utilized, including HUD-FHA mortgage insurance programs, conventional financing, and tax-exempt
bonds or other obligations. If the Housing Assistance Payment Contract is pledged as security for any loan or obligation, the financing
must be approved by HUD.

The rents approved under the Contract (Contract Rents) may not
exceed the HUD-established Fair Market Rents for new construction
for the housing market area in which the project will be located and
must be reasonable in relation to the quality, location, amenities,
methods, and terms of financing and to the management and maintenance services to the project. The Fair Market Rents may be exceeded
by up to 10 percent in cases in which the field office director determines that special circumstances so warrant and the rents meet the
test of reasonableness. The Fair Market Rents may be exceeded by
up to 20 percent in cases in which the assistant secretary for housing
production and mortgage credit determines that special circumstances
so warrant or determines that such higher rents are necessary to the
implementation of a Housing Assistance Plan.

The initial Contract Rents for projects that will be financed by
FHA mortgage insurance may not exceed the rents approved by HUD
in connection with the mortgage insurance for the project.

Contract Rents to the owner will be adjusted annually by the HUD-
established Automatic Annual Adjustment Factor. Special additional
adjustments may be approved to reflect actual and necessary expenses
of owning and maintaining the project that have resulted from substantial general increases in real property taxes, utility rates, or similar
costs (assessments, and utilities not covered by regulated rates), but
only to the extent that such general increases are not compensated for
by the Automatic Annual Adjustments.

The maximum term for the Contract is 20 years, or 40 years
in the case of a project owned or financed by a loan or a loan guarantee
from a state or local agency. The actual term will be established on
the basis of the amount of capital expenditures reasonably required
for the project, the reasonable rate and period of amortization for the
financing, and the approved rents to the owner.

The owner will be responsible for performance of all maintenance
and management functions (including taking of applications, selection
of families, collection of rents, termination of tenancies, reexamina-

tion of family income, and compliance with equal opportunity requirements). In connection with the selection of families, the owner is responsible for leasing at least 30 percent of the units to very-low-income families (families whose income does not exceed 50 percent of
the median income for the locality). Subject to HUD approval, the
owner may contract with another entity to perform such services,
provided the management contract will not shift any of the owner's re-
sponsibilities or obligations. However, no entity that is responsible
for administration of the Contract (for example, a Public Housing Administration [PHA] in the case of a private-owner/PHA project) may
contract to perform such services.

Private owners may also participate in the Section 8 program by
leasing existing decent, safe, and sanitary housing to lower-income
families. Under this program, a family that has been determined
eligible by the PHA will be given a Certificate of Family Participation.
The family may then seek a suitable unit anywhere within the operating
jurisdiction of the PHA. If the owner is willing to lease a unit and
the unit is determined to be in decent, safe, and sanitary condition,
and if the gross rent is within the HUD-established Fair Market Rent
for existing housing, a lease may be executed between the owner and
the family and a Housing Assistance Payments Contract will be executed between the PHA and the owner. This contract will assure a monthly
payment to the owner in an amount sufficient to make up the differences
between the rent payable by the family and the Contract Rent to the
owner.

A separate set of regulations has been developed for State Housing Finance and Development Agencies (HFAs), now present in 32
states. Most HFAs provide below-market interest rate financing to
private developers of low- and moderate-income housing. The regulations permit qualified agencies to receive "set-asides"—earmarkings
of Section 8 contract authority that the HFA can allocate generally according to its own housing program. In addition, agencies that provide financing without federal mortgage insurance are permitted a
greater degree of program responsibility, such as the selection of the
developer (either by advertising or negotiation), approval of design
and construction quality, site selection, economic feasibility, and
marketability. The Section 8 subsidy payments with respect to an
HFA-financed project are computed and disbursed in the same manner
as for the basic program, and the Housing Assistance Payments Contract term for an HFA-financed project may be up to 40 years.

Section-8 Leased-Housing Program
Questions and Answers

What Is the Section 8 Leased Housing Program?

This is a new program provided for by the 1974 Housing and
Community Development Act that is in effect the only federal housing
subsidy program. The Leased Housing Program, or Housing Assistance Payments Program, as it is also known, is a program of privately constructed, privately financed housing with 20 to 100 percent
of the units to receive Housing Assistance Payments that reduce the
rent paid by tenants to 15 to 25 percent of income.

Is This a New-Construction Program?

Yes, but new construction and rehabilitation is used only in
communities that do not have a sufficient supply of suitable existing
units. The existing-housing program does not operate under the procedures set forth here.

How Are Section 8 Projects Financed?

Section 8 is a subsidy program, not a finance program. Financing may be conventional, HUD insured, or a direct loan from a state
HFA. The latter, where available, offers the most attractive opportunities. Bond financing, similar to the old Section 23 program, is
also permitted.

What Are the Income Limits for Family
Eligibility to Occupy Section 8 Units?

This program is designed to house lower-income and very-low-
income families. The act defines lower-income families as those whose
income does not exceed 80 percent of the median income for the area.
Very-low-income families have incomes that do not exceed 50 percent
of the median income for the area. At least 30 percent of any project
must be leased to very-low-income families.

Who Determines Median Income Eligibility?

HUD will establish median income figures for each geographic
area, with adjustments for smaller or larger families. HUD may
establish income limits lower or higher than 80 percent of median if
it finds that variations are necessary in a particular area due to construction costs, unusually high or low incomes, or other factors.

How Much Rent Does the Tenant Pay?

Eligible tenants pay 15 to 25 percent of their income. Most families will pay 25 percent of their gross income as rent. Large families and those with unusually high medical or other expenses will pay 15 percent of their gross income as rent. The housing assistance payment makes up the difference between the tenant's rent and the full contract or economic rent.

Who Receives the Housing Assistance Payment?

As in the rent supplement program, the owner receives the Federal Housing Assistance Payment. The Housing Assistance Payment together with the rent paid by the tenant equals the total Contract Rent.

How Are Developers Selected?

Those state housing development agencies that have the capability of making direct nonfederally insured loans will be given separate set-asides of funds and broad authority to administer the program. The procedures here will not be very different from present 236 projects done on a direct basis with state housing development agencies.

The HUD field offices will advertise for proposals asking for a certain number of units and a certain mix in a locality (the offering may be for a large number of units with multiple proposals to be accepted). The announcement will state maximum Fair Market Rents. Proposals are to be preliminary in nature with data on proposed unit sizes, rent, equipment, and utilities together with financials and information on site, location, development team, and sponsor. A sketch of site, building, and unit plans is also to be provided. The concept is for this to be a basic and relatively inexpensive proposal to prepare. The Local Housing Authority may submit a proposal in response to HUD's announcement.

How Will HUD Review and Select Proposals?

Proposals will be reviewed by HUD and ranked. (State HFAs will make their own selection of development proposals.) In the case of projects of 50 or more units that are not for the elderly, preference will be given to those projects providing for 20 percent or less of the units to be subsidized. HUD expects most proposals to be on a 100 percent basis. Consideration will be given to the rent proposed, but this will not necessarily be awarded on a low-bid basis. In making its selections, HUD will look for the best combination of rent, site, and previous experience of the developer, taking into account any comments of local and area government.

What Are the Maximum Project Rents for This Program?

HUD has determined Fair Market Rents for each community for different size and types of unit (garden, detached, townhouse, elevator). These rents include all utilities and are trended for two years to cover the period of development and construction. Rents for units designed for the elderly and the handicapped are the Fair Market Rents for the applicable type of unit multiplied by a factor of 1.05.

Is There Any Way Fair Market Rents Can Be Increased?

Area office directors may increase Fair Market Rents by up to 10 percent if special circumstances so warrant and if the higher rent is reasonable in terms of the housing being provided. The HUD central office may authorize an increase of up to 20 percent. This is a new program, and further adjustments in Fair Market Rents may be required on a special basis to eliminate inequities.

What Rents Should Developers Propose?

Since there is currently little if any opportunity to increase rents and subsidies during processing, most developers will file proposals at maximum, or at least at rents that provide an adequate margin for contingencies and increases during construction. However, HUD may counterpropose if it believes that the site and overall proposal do not justify maximum rents.

How Are Projects Requiring HUD-Insured Mortgages Processed?

Developers contemplating HUD financing will file Site and Market Analysis (SAMA) applications (without fee) simultaneously with their Section 8 preliminary proposals to HUD. The preliminary reservation of Section 8 funds for these projects will be accompanied by a SAMA (with fee) and proceed with HUD processing in anticipation of future Section 8 assistance. Such advance processing may be conditioned upon subsequent approval of Section 8 assistance.

Are Housing Assistance (Subsidy) Payments Considered in Underwriting for HUD-Insured Mortgages?

Yes. HUD mortgage insurance underwriting must meet marketability tests, but the number of units for which housing assistance payments are to be made available will be considered by HUD as an addition to the effective demand for unassisted rental units.

What About an Escalator for Increased Costs?

There are automatic annual adjustments in rent based upon a HUD-determined percentage charge in Fair Market Rent in the area. HUD may also authorize additional adjustments to cover substantial general increases in taxes or utilities. There are provisions for increased subsidies to meet these increased rents.

What Is the Term of the Contract for Housing Assistance Payments?

The term is basically 20 years for new construction and rehabilitation but 40 years for projects financed by state HFAs.

Are Minimum Property Standards a Requirement of the Section 8 New-Construction Program?

Yes.

Are Davis-Bacon Prevailing Wages a Requirement of Section 8?

Yes.

Who Manages the Completed Project?

The owner is responsible for the management of the property, and management fees are included in the Fair Market Rent. In some cases, this may be contracted to the public housing authority, and local housing authorities can themselves serve as developers.

What about Unoccupied Units?

During rent-up and in cases in which a tenant breaks a lease, HUD will pay 80 percent of the Contract Rent for a period of 60 days. Otherwise, the owner bears the risk of unoccupied units. Even in a project in which 100 percent of the units are under a contract for housing assistance payments, such payments are made only for units that are actually occupied. Therefore, the prospective developer must assure himself that there is a demand for the units.

When Will the Program Be Operational?

Regulations for each program, Fair Market Rent tables, and the like have been published. While some further changes or refinements are likely, project processing is operational now.

How Big Is This Program?

Some 400,000 units are provided for under the act, to be divided among new, rehabilitated, and existing housing.

Section 202 Housing Program for the Elderly

The Section 202 housing program for the elderly had been phased out in the late 1960s but was reinstituted in 1975 as a construction program for nonprofit sponsors of housing for the elderly. The current regulations do provide a direct construction loan to eligible sponsors at the Treasury interest rate. The permanent financing can be provided by an acceptable HUD-insured program, such as Section 221(d)(3) Market Interest Rate or Section 231, by a state HFA direct loan, or by other financing routes acceptable to HUD. Although there is some confusion at this time whether Section 202 will also be made to provide permanent financing as well as construction monies, there is one distinct advantage to the program in that Section 8 lease subsidies are tied directly to the 202 loan and could provide such assistance for up to 100 percent of the units.

Other Housing Programs

Ongoing rural housing programs will be outlined later on in this chapter. Other HUD programs are available for the development of nursing homes with a 90 percent insured loan (Section 232) and the development of conventional housing (Section 207), but our primary interest here is in those who require below-market rents to afford decent housing. For family and senior citizen housing, Section 8 is the only current option on the federal level, and the state HFAs need to be contacted to determine if their current interest rates will provide financing for your needs.

FINDING NEW WAYS TO FINANCE HOUSING

There is much discussion among ICH participants and other organizations concerned about decent housing about finding new, innovative financing methods so that those desiring to provide needed housing are not so dependent on a few limited governmental programs.

Within your own investigation of imaginative financing possibilities, you might invite a person familiar with Bond Programs to help you determine if you have the base for such financing. Or you might confer with your local lenders to see if they might combine a social sensitivity with interest rates realistic to needed rent structures. Or you could explore with local financiers or with the National Housing Partnerships to determine if a combination of your nonprofit status and their monies could produce a limited partnership arrangement that could make a project feasible.

The following is an attorney's view of how the nonprofit organization can work within a limited dividend sponsorship.

As a result of changes in the Internal Revenue Code, investment in governmentally subsidized multifamily housing has become one of the most attractive tax shelters available to wealthy investors. No attempt will be made here to describe the intricacies of the tax shelter; suffice it to say that carefully developed projects have netted investors anywhere from 15 to 35 percent on their investment.

Recently, nonprofit organizations have begun to examine possible ways that they could use the limited profit (also known as limited dividend) development route in lieu of the 100 percent financed nonprofit route.

There are several reasons why a nonprofit organization would use this approach. First, in high-cost areas, where 10 percent of the development costs can be obtained from investors, projects are more likely to be economically feasible within the federal statutory limits. Second, nonprofit organizations are always short of funds for social service programs within the developments, as well as for organizational and administrative expenses required as a sponsor. By using the limited profit route, they have been able to generate funds from the sales of the depreciation tax shelter, which would otherwise go unused. And third, by using the limited profit, the nonprofit organization can exercise major control over the development, provide services to the tenants, and provide the project with a relationship to the local neighborhood, and at the same time avoid the liability of direct ownership responsibility.

The nonprofit organization will enter into an arrangement with a builder-developer-sponsor whereby it establishes a legal relationship to the project in return for its sharing in some of the funds generated by the development. These projects are generally developed by the use of a partnership, with a general partner responsible for the development and management of the project as well as for liability for the debts of the development. The general partner (which may or may not be a corporation) enters into a relationship with one or more limited partners, who have bought into the project solely for investment purposes and have no liability for its general debts and whose primary interest is to obtain the benefits of the tax shelter that the project generates. The limited partners are usually wealthy individuals in high tax brackets who need tax losses to offset taxable income.

The nonprofit organization's main interest is to encourage needed housing produced in its community as well as seeing to it that the subsequent residents are adequately served through community-type programs.

The nonprofit organization may have a variety of relationships to the project. It may become involved because it has control of a site through urban renewal designation or land already owned or optioned to it, or because of the power that its prestige as a community group gives it in determining the success or failure of a development in a particular neighborhood. Its leverage is thus control of a site and community approval and support.

It may arrange to be a general partner or to have a formal tie to the general partner, either by having membership on the board, or, in some cases, being assigned the status of a "special partner." This is a rather legally ill-defined relationship and must be carefully explored in reference to local partnership laws. The advantage that this status gives the nonprofit organization is access to the books and records of the partnership and thus full knowledge of the development, though its control of the general partner will always be less than majority control in such an arrangement. In any event, the exact relationship has to be carefully worked out in order to avoid jeopardizing the exempt status of the nonprofit entity; the Agreement of Limited Partnership will define the necessary parameters.

The nonprofit organization could also have a contractual relationship with the partnership to provide program services and community support for the project without having any formal relationship with the partnership.

Utilizing either of the last two ties, the nonprofit organization may share in the following items of profit that the project may generate:

1. It may share in a proportionate return on equity allowed by HUD. This is a maximum of 6 percent and is usually not considered a significant cash generation feature by the investors. Where arrangements for sharing this item are made, the nonprofit organization usually cannot take more than a 50 percent share; otherwise, the development could be considered by the IRS as one that is not a business venture, but rather one entered into merely to generate tax losses and thus not a for-profit venture. It may be preferable for tax purposes for the nonprofit organization to enter into a contractual arrangement with the developer to provide specific services to the project in consideration for its sharing in the return on equity.

2. Since wealthy taxpayers are able, for a comparatively small cash investment, to deduct the entire development cost of the project from their tax returns, and since this is a very valuable tax shelter device, with shares in premium that may run from 1 to 10 percent above the 10 percent cash requirement, the nonprofit organization may

be able to negotiate a sharing of the profit made on the sale of the
equity. Arrangements have been made that give the nonprofit organization between one-third and one-half of the profits on the sale of the
equity. This may come in the form of either a lump sum payment or
annual contributions over the depreciable life of the investment.

3. Nonprofit organizations may be able to negotiate a share of
any profits generated by appreciation in the value of the project at the
time of its sale after the tax shelter advantage has been used up by
the initial investors.

4. Nonprofit organizations may negotiate an arrangement that
permits them the first right to purchase the project from the initial
investors once the tax shelter has been used up. Coop conversion may
well be the first option, with sale to the nonprofit entity the second.
The nonprofit organization may be able to negotiate a relatively firm
arrangement with the developer and with HUD to have the project re-
financed on a nonprofit basis at the time the initial investors are ready
to pull out.

5. The nonprofit organization should negotiate control over
management, including the picking of the management firm. In a
well-run project, income from management can be an important consideration as well as a local neighborhood business opportunity for
minority or poverty groups.

Thus, in considering whether or not to sponsor a housing development under one of the governmental programs, the limited profit
route is one that should be carefully considered by any potential sponsoring group. Failure to do so can result in the loss of potential revenue by the nonprofit organization as well as the loss of service revenue for the residents. There are additional needs to this process and
they can only be overcome by the expertise of skilled tax and legal
financial consultants.

In addition to the fact that the limited profit route can generate
cash flow for the sponsoring nonprofit group, churches and other nonprofit sponsoring groups could look to their membership for the provision of funds for development. There are often members in the organization who are in high tax brackets. The organization could develop
the necessary sophistication to convince these members that there are
opportunities for them to obtain excellent tax shelter investment opportunities while at the same time enable the organization to fulfill its
humanitarian commitment to provide housing for low- and moderate-
income families.

This opportunity for development exists for any multifamily new
construction, whether for the elderly or for families with children.
This provides another area of opportunity for the nonprofit development
seeking to meet the lower/moderate-income housing needs in its community.

THE APPLICATION PROCESS

If you have chosen a HUD-insured program and you will be submitting your application and exhibits to your local HUD area office, the process could go through three possible application stages—feasibility, conditional, and firm. The conditional application stage is often bypassed. If you are going through your state HFA and a direct-loan program, the application process is similar in the first stage but has local variables in the next stages. If a more conventional financing route has been established and you are obtaining a direct loan through a local lending institution, your application for loan will be negotiated by local customs and banking regulations.

Whatever your housing development program and financing route, you will probably have a preliminary application meeting with the insuring or lending agency at which the process will be explained and blank forms issued. Some variation of the following exhibits will be required in the early application submission:

1. Application showing costs, rents, and mortgage required
2. Equal Employment Opportunity certification indicating you will hire without discrimination as to race, creed, or national origin
3. Previous participation certificate indicating what housing developments you have been involved in in the past
4. Housing consultant contract
5. Corporation's financial statement
6. Narrative to indicate eligibility as a nonprofit sponsor
7. Affirmative marketing plans showing how advertising and rent-up will work to ensure fair housing opportunities
8. Location map of site showing the surrounding streets and nature of the neighborhood
9. Boundary map and plot plan showing the site size and the location of the proposed building
10. Evidence of site control and a legal description of the site
11. Evidence of a market for your project units
12. Zoning map and ordinance to indicate that you have the proper zoning
13. Environmental information describing the impact the project will have on the environment
14. Evidence of water and sewage facilities for the project
15. Proposed management plan
16. Brief specifications of the architect's early determinations

The insuring or financing agency wants to see that you are serious about your intent to develop a housing project, that you have the necessary expertise to accomplish it, and that local conditions warrant the project. The agency or institution will then process your application and exhibits.

Once the application has been dropped, you will be given some kind of receipt saying that it has been received. There will be a waiting period of 30 to 60 days while the agency makes its own feasibility checks of your proposal. Your application and exhibits will be divided and sent in all directions to the responsible departments within the agency:

1. Real Estate and Valuation Section: Where is the site? What is it near? Is it worth it?

2. Cost Section: Do the costs add up? Does it look economically feasible?

3. Finance and Mortgage Credit Section: Does it fit our program? Can we underwrite this project?

4. Architectural and Engineering Section: Do the preliminary plans meet the minimum property standard? Will the site sustain the type of structure requested?

5. Housing Management Section: Does the management plan indicate a sensitive understanding of the prospective tenants? Does the management look professional and able to keep a project solvent?

6. Equal Opportunity Section: Will minorities have an equal chance to work on this project?

7. Environmental Section: Is the environmental impact of the proposed project within the allowable limits?

8. Economic and Market Analysis Section: Will people rent in this proposed project at the rents indicated?

These or similar sections will make independent findings, then come together and talk about the overall project and make recommendations for changes or for an out-and-out rejection or acceptance until the program chief is able to make a recommendation to the director. You will receive either a go or a no-go letter from the director.

Often either changes are required or the proposed project is rejected because of matters that one section or another could not approve. In this case you and your consultant and appropriate members of the development team request meetings with the officials who can review these matters with you. Rely on your consultant to establish these contacts. Go as a team to show your solidarity. You will find that the expertise of your development team will start to unravel any misunderstandings that might exist between the agency personnel and your submitted exhibits. Usually a meeting of the minds will occur at such meetings and the basis for resubmission developed. Keep the lines of communication open.

If an impasse with the agency should develop over issues that do not seem germane or substantive or if hidden agencies seem to be blocking a logical processing of your project, you may wish to seek political advice from local, state, or federal government officials. Your consultant may suggest this route as a last resort in order for your project to receive the proper attention. You may suggest this route to your consultant from a broader knowledge of your local political situation. Do not make moves in this direction without each other. Keep a balanced relationship. Do not panic. Continue to work as a team. If the political advice route is the way to go, it will become evident.

Because you are committed, you have a basically sound development plan, you have surrounded yourself with experts, and you are persistent, you have finally received a letter approving your project at the feasibility level and are invited to submit at the next appropriate application stage.

During this period, the full architectural design will emerge. The following questions you might want to keep in mind for your project design review have been developed by a Housing Development Corporation Sponsor Development Curriculum.

The review and evaluation of the plans should reflect the goals of the organization and should be based on the effect that this design will have on the residents of the development.

1. Is the land being used to the best possible advantage? Are the number of units per acre in the best interests of the residents?

2. Is the arrangement of units acceptable in appearance to the community?

3. Will the landscape plan provide for the use of existing trees located on the property?

4. Is the drainage system such that sidewalks, yards, doorways, and so on will not be flooded in a heavy rain?

5. Are the garbage disposal areas placed so that they are not unattractive to the residents and the community?

6. Are the parking spaces adequate for each building?

7. Are the play areas located so that they are convenient to all of the units and will not disturb the residents closest to the areas?

8. Are the units arranged so that there is a mixture of sizes in the same building? Are the three- and four-bedroom apartments scattered throughout the project?

9. Is there adequate space for storage, closets, pantry, and so on?

10. Is room layout and circulation convenient for the residents? (For example, is the eating area close to the kitchen area? Is the bath close to the bedrooms?)

11. Are doors and windows placed so that the furniture space can be utilized to the maximum?

12. Do the doors open in a way that is convenient?

13. Is there exterior space that is usable (for example, porch or patio)?

14. Are there bath fans where there are no windows?

15. Do the bathrooms have shower fixtures?

16. Are there exhaust fans in the kitchens?

In addition to the sponsor's desires, the architect must be certain that the plans reflect certain features required by FHA:

1. The site must be clear of hazardous conditions, such as smoke, possible flooding, and odors.

2. The condition of the soil, ground water level, drainage, and so on must be acceptable.

3. Access to the property must be available.

4. Local codes and regulations must be adhered to, if these codes are more stringent than the FHA codes.

5. The boundary of the property must be correct; the survey must be conducted by a reliable engineer.

6. Utilities must be available and sufficient for each unit.

7. The property must be designed so that the units and other buildings can be used without trespassing on adjoining properties.

8. Each living unit must have provisions for each of the following:

  a. a continuing supply of safe and potable water
  b. sanitary facilities and a safe method of sewage disposal
  c. heating adequate for healthful and comfortable living conditions
  d. electricity for lighting and for equipment used in the dwelling
  e. adequate provisions for the removal of garbage and trash and its sanitary storage pending removal

Once your architect has developed working drawings and working specifications (exact, measured design and material input) that are acceptable to you and to the insuring or financing agency and local ordinances, the general contractor can take the plans and specifications for costing by subcontractors who will bid on their specialties required in the proposed project. The final budget of the general contractor, based on these accumulated bids and his own requirements, overhead, and profit, must correspond to the total construction amounts used on the application for funding. Once this has been accomplished, the final application stage has been reached.

To reach this stage you have conquered more obstacles than you thought were involved. Now, after compromise yet with firm follow-through toward the housing goal first envisioned, your entire development team has come through with required exhibits to be added to the exhibits previously submitted. These include an updated application reflecting current interest rates, revised costs, final expense, tax, and rents (you will pay a required percentage of the mortgage for an application fee); the architect's working drawings and working specifications; and the general contractor's costing of plans as trade breakdown costs. With agency approval of these plans and costs, you will be invited through a letter of firm commitment for your project to gather all required documents for the initial closing, at which time allowable funds will be dispersed and construction financing will be finalized.

Moving toward the start of construction, which is just beyond the stage called initial closing, you will feel both the excitement of anticipation and the frustration of finding there are still loose ends and unanticipated hurdles before closing can be achieved.

No one can tell you exactly what they will be. The problems will be peculiar to your situation. Just be prepared to tackle the problems with the same persistence that brought you this far. Expect the unexpected. Perhaps the builder cannot find bond. In such a case, you may have to find an alternative to bonding—perhaps working through a letter of credit or finding a new builder at the last minute. A utility company may not provide services. Your architect may then have to rework the energy source. This will change cost and rents. The mortgage will have to be reworked. A revised commitment will have to be sought. Perhaps the local government has just declared a sewer moratorium. Depending upon earlier sewer connection commitments, you may need to work out a new agreement through legal assistance. Stay with it. What if the interest rate changes? Such changes are rarely more than half of 1 percent—enough to change numbers up and down the line. A revised application is in order. Work it through. Perhaps the building permit has been stalled. This is a common time problem. Encourage the builder to start the process for the permit as soon as possible. You will need it at closing.

You can count on problems like these. Just be aware that non-profit developers have developed thousands of new and rehabilitated housing units in our country. They had problems and they solved them.

Often it will seem to you as if the world is run by forms. It helps to know that the attorney will work up the technical requirements for all the forms and exhibits needed for closing. The list of closing documents is formidable and a partial list is included here to indicate that your attorney has work to do that requires the cooperation of the entire development team:

1. agency commitment
2. assignment of commitment
3. list of financial requirements for closing
4. application for insurance of advance (if required)
5. contractor's requisition and prevailing wage certificate (if required)
6. mortgagor's and architect's certificate
7. regulatory agreement
8. articles of incorporation
9. bylaws
10. minutes of meeting of directors, including authorizing resolutions
11. certificate of incumbency
12. zoning compliance letter
13. building permit
14. survey plat
15. surveyor's report
16. mortgagee's title insurance policy
17. deed of trust note
18. deed of trust
19. building loan agreement
20. construction contract
21. performance bond
22. payment bond
23. owner-architect agreement
24. memorandum of insurance
25. assurances of utility services
26. contractor's and/or mortagagor's cost breakdown
27. mortgagee's certificate
28. mortgagor's certificate
29. assurance of compliance with Civil Rights Act
30. mortgagor's oath
31. contractor's certification
32. mortgagor's attorney's opinion
33. agreement and certification
34. security agreement
35. financing statement
36. request for preliminary determination of eligibility as nonprofit
37. certificate of relationships and nonprofit motives
38. architect's certification
39. attorney's certification
40. general contractor's certification
41. management agent's certification
42. sponsor's certification
43. management contract

Fortified with all those completed documents, the entire development team gathers at the closing table, executes the final forms, and disperses the necessary monies for land purchase and fees to the consultant, architect, attorney, and title insurance agent. The builder now has money in the bank from which to make construction draws as necessary and can start work immediately.

CONSTRUCTION

Being a sidewalk superintendent can be fun, as long as you do not move from the sidewalk into the construction site to dispense your building wisdom. Your enthusiasm is understandable, but remember that you have engaged a supervising architect to serve as your representative during construction. He will protect your interests on the site.

Many a development team has been subjected to unneeded stress when overanxious sponsors interfered in the construction process with suggestions or demands not printed in the blueprints and not part of the job as costed out by the builder. The sponsor should expect strict adherence to the plans and to sound building practices. If something seems out of phase, the supervising architect is the one to question; it is he who should follow through on your questions and observations.

Sometimes change orders are required to add, remove, or change some part of the structure from the way it was in the plans. You should have a definitive say in any such decision. What will it cost? What is the time factor? Questions such as these will determine that decision.

The general contractor has agreed in the contract with you to build your project within a set period of time—probably 12, 18, or 24 months, depending on the size and type of structure. The construction loan is also arranged for that period of time. It is essential at this stage that time schedules be met. If there is a time overrun, then there will not be enough interest money in the mortgage and additional payroll funds will be required, but the construction holdback (money not released until final closing) prevents the general contractor from access to this money for payment to subcontractors, who may not get paid and may not work until paid, and additional time delays will result.

Delays in construction and in the final closing of the construction loan create unexpected money problems that seem to compound themselves. Be aware of time in respect to construction and final closing of the loan. If there seems to be a gap in progress, discuss it with your supervising architect.

Sometimes there occur what can be called "unavoidable delays" —things your general contractor seems to have no control over. It could be a strike by union workers over grievances on another job, a delay in materials, or unusual weather conditions. When such delays occur, it is important that your supervising architect document them for a later request to increase the time of the contract with a concurrent increase in mortgage monies to complete the construction with the required additional construction money. Your consultant will assist you in your application for such increases.

It is also important to recognize that, even when construction is completed on time, the construction loan is not closed until all required closing documents are completed and approved. Your consultant and closing attorney will need your cooperation and that of the general contractor to gather the required exhibits and present them in the proper order to the insuring or financing agency. With the excitement of a completed building, tenants moving in, and accolades coming in from admiring supporters, it is not easy to move once again through a mountain of paperwork. It is an effort that must be expedited with all deliberate speed, since the construction interest rate clock is still running. When there is final closing and you have a long-term mortgage payable by rents, then it is time to rest on your laurels. In the meantime, get yourself to the closing on time.

Finally, after the two, three, four, or more years that have passed since you first saw the need, you have become part of the solution. The dedication ceremony is a time for community leaders, sponsors and friends, the development team, and tenants to join in mutual thanksgiving. In the afterglow, you could even decide to look around and begin another project.

MANAGEMENT

In order for lower-income housing programs to provide meaningful services to families and appropriate rewards to owners, the tenants must become deeply involved in the problem. In this way, many of the factors that cause hopelessness and depression among such residents can be at least ameliorated. Participation can lead to a rich family experience beyond the feeling of paid-up rent or a freshly mowed lawn.

The integration of families in a community program does not mean that their individual family responsibility is preempted. It should provide for a continuing education in the social, economic, interpersonal, recreational, and spiritual life of families. This is particularly important because many lower-income families have had little opportunity to develop a sense of pride in themselves as individuals, family units, or a community.

What people think of themselves is of crucial importance. It is one of the determining factors in motivating families and individuals

HUNT LIBRARY
CARNEGIE-MELLON UNIVERSITY
PITTSBURGH, PENNSYLVANIA 15213

to utilize their own ability to better their circumstances. Parent attitudes of hopelessness are transmitted to their children, and by involving the families in a developmental program of building a spirit of community, the attitude of "what's the use" could give way to one of pride in self, family, and community.

Housing is not enough to meet the basic needs of poor America. There must be, in addition, a program of economic, social, cultural, and educational development that meets their other needs. The style of management that your organization is committed to develop should seek to include this wider interpretation in the lower- and moderate-income housing field.

There are many ways in which this style of management can become meaningful. Families can become involved in significant projects that underline their individual and family identities as responsible citizens who participate in community life. A community council can be developed that offers open participation in the decision-making processes and creates opportunities for meaningful relationships among families and between tenants and management. Public and private agencies can become involved, which can bring resources to the needs of tenants and help them to achieve a fuller and more satisfying life. Sound business management not only ensures the financial success of the project, including paying all obligations, but it carries over into the responsible action of the tenant in prompt payment of rent and sharing in the pride that comes from participating in the maintenance of attractive and safe housing. Finally, supplemental opportunities can aid in individual or family growth and development, such as well-baby clinics, health services, planned parenthood, budget planning, nutrition classes, sewing classes, tutoring of children and adults, recreation, and a thrift shop.

RURAL HOUSING DEVELOPMENT

When most people think about poor housing in the United States, they generally think about the slums and deteriorating neighborhoods in Chicago, New York, Los Angeles, and other metropolitan areas where the problems are most visible. Seldom do they realize that, even though there is a serious urban housing problem that needs further attention and resources, the housing problem in rural America is much worse.

The 1970 Census of Housing revealed that, of the 20 million households residing in nonmetropolitan areas, almost 2.5 million lived in substandard dwellings, that is, those lacking essential plumbing facilities consisting of a toilet, a bathtub or a shower, and hot and cold piped water inside the structure. This means that 56 percent

of the 4.4 million households occupying substandard housing in the
United States are located in nonmetropolitan areas that make up only
31 percent of the total population. Or, to put it another way, 12 out
every 100 rural (nonmetropolitan) households lived in substandard
housing, compared with only 3 out of every 100 in metropolitan areas.
Thus, the housing situation is worse, both quantitatively and relatively,
in rural America.

Several factors emerge from an examination of the relevant
statistics. First, as one would expect, poor people are most likely
to live in poor housing. Less than 5 percent of households reporting
incomes between $7,000 and $10,000 lived in housing that lacked
plumbing or was severely overcrowded; more than 15 percent of households with incomes of less than $4,000 lacked decent housing. Thus,
there is a clear inverse relationship between income and adequate
housing. Recognizing that 44 percent of the poverty households are
located in nonmetropolitan areas, it is not surprising that a disproportionate amount of the bad housing exists in these same areas. Thus,
any serious attempt to deal with the overall housing problem must include a means for redistributing income so that lower-income families
will be able to secure housing that they cannot now afford.

Another obvious reason for poor housing is racial discrimination. In nonmetropolitan areas, 49 percent of black families with incomes between $4,000 and $6,000 occupied housing that lacked plumbing or was severely overcrowded, but only 12 percent of nonblack families in the same income category lived in this kind of housing. Thus,
enforcement of civil rights in housing must be an essential ingredient
of any serious proposal to meet rural housing needs.

Beyond income, there is a clear relationship between geography
and decent housing. There is a difference not only from one region of
the country to another, but also between rural areas and small towns
and the nation's urban communities. For families in the $4,000-to-
$7,000 income bracket living in metropolitan areas, the incidence of
bad housing was about 6 percent; for families in the same income category living in nonmetropolitan areas, the incidence was nearly 14 percent.

The reasons behind this disparity and the general failure to establish an effective rural housing program are a reflection of the adequacy of public institutions and the private market system in rural
areas. Recognizing that housing credit institutions are primarily
metropolitan in terms of location and orientation, it is not surprising
that there is a severe housing credit gap in most rural areas and
small towns. As a result, the major federal housing programs under
HUD, which are almost totally dependent on private financing, have
not functioned very effectively in nonmetropolitan areas. Similarly,
as evidence of the institutional gap in rural areas, approximately 50

percent of the counties in the United States, containing some 40 million
persons, were still without any public housing program as of 1971.
Thus, even when the credit gap could be circumvented, many counties
did not establish instructions to take advantage of the resources available, particularly with regard to low-income housing development.

FEDERAL PROGRAMS AND RESOURCES FOR
RURAL HOUSING NEEDS

To partly offset these special credit and institutional problems,
nonmetropolitan America does have its own housing agency, FmHA,
which is a division of the Department of Agriculture. This agency does
not serve all nonmetropolitan areas, however, as it is restricted by
statute to rural areas and cities with a population of 20,000 or less.
(It should be noted, however, that FmHA is currently refusing to make
its services available to cities with populations of over 10,000 on the
basis that it needs more staff to serve the additional jurisdictions
authorized in the 1974 housing act.)

Although FmHA and HUD programs are similar (recognizing
that most HUD-subsidized housing programs are in a state of limbo
since the Nixon administration impounded most of its funds in 1973),
there are two important differences to keep in mind. First, FmHA
is not dependent on local financial institutions for mortgage credit,
but instead originates loans out of its own Rural Housing Insurance
Fund. Second, FmHA has approximately 1,700 offices serving every
county in the United States. This means that potential borrowers (individuals, nonprofit organizations, and other eligible parties) deal
directly with FmHA officials at the county level and have direct access to mortgage funds. Although this is not to say there are no problems in working with FmHA, it is much simpler and easier than the
complicated network of FHA.

In determining which FmHA programs are suitable to the low-
income housing needs in your particular area, it should be recognized
that, in addition to the statutory restraints mentioned above, there is
a substantial number of families and individuals that are not and cannot be served by FmHA due to their inadequate incomes, or, better
stated, the inadequacy of the housing subsidies authorized by Congress.
Prior to 1975, as indicated in reports on FmHA housing assistance
programs over the past few years, families earning less than a $3,000
adjusted income annually (gross income less $300 per dependent) were
not eligible for any kind of housing assistance from FmHA. This in effect means that approximately 1.6 million out of 3.1 million households
in FmHA's jurisdiction that are in need of improved housing cannot be
served due to the restraints and limitations of the current housing programs.

With the passage of the 1974 housing act, which included new authorities and deeper subsidies for low-income housing programs administered by FmHA, there were more opportunities to meet the housing needs of senior citizens, migrant and other farmworkers, and other low-income rural Americans.

The following is a brief description of the various FmHA housing loan and grant programs.

Section 502

Section 502 is FmHA's largest housing program, with an appropriation of $2.1 billion in fiscal year 1975 for the financing of approximately 100,000 new and existing housing units for low- and moderate-income families. At least 50 percent of these funds are required by law to be utilized for low-income families with adjusted incomes of $8,500 annually or less.

This program provides loans for the following purposes: to construct, improve, or relocate a dwelling; to buy a building site; to buy a house and lot; to provide a water supply and sewage disposal facilities; to modernize a home by adding bathrooms, central heating, and modern kitchens, including a range, refrigerator, clothes washer, and clothes dryer; to provide foundation plantings and seeding or sodding of lawns; to buy and improve homes for farm laborers; to refinance debts under certain conditions; to pay legal expenses.

Interest rates vary from 8.125 percent down to 1 percent. Up to 33 years are allowed to repay. Loans of more than $2,500 and loans to be repaid in more than 10 years must be secured by a mortgage on the house and lot. Loans of not more than $2,500 scheduled for repayment within 10 years may be secured by a promissory note.

Those who may qualify include rural residents, farmers, and urban residents who want to live in the country. In addition, applicants must be without decent, safe, and sanitary housing and be unable to obtain the needed credit from other sources at reasonable rates and terms. The maximum adjusted income that applicants can have and still qualify for loans is $12,900, except in Hawaii and Alaska.

Housing must be located in open country or in towns with a population of not more than 20,000. The size of the house is limited to 1,300 square feet of living space, except for large families. An applicant whose income is not sufficient to repay a rural housing loan may be able to obtain a loan if a relative or someone else with adequate repayment ability cosigns his note. The only cost in applying for an FmHA loan is the cost of a credit report. However, if the application is approved, the applicant pays for legal services necessary to make certain he has a satisfactory title to the land and for other loan closing

costs. These costs can be included in the loans, and houses can be
built on leased land. (For further information see FmHA Instruction
444.1. Also see Code of Federal Regulations at 7 CFR 1822.1 through
1822.15.)

Low-income individuals and families (those with adjusted annual
incomes of $8,500 or less) who receive Section 502 housing loans may
be eligible for interest credits that will reduce the effective interest
rate to as low as 1 percent. The amount of interest credit depends on
income and size of family. Houses built with the aid of interest credit
loans must be modest in design and contain no more than 1,300 square
feet, except for large families. Interest credit agreements are reviewed every two years and the amount of the interest credit increased
or reduced in line with any change in the family's income or number of
children. (For further information on interest credits, see FmHA
Instruction 444.1 or request a copy of the Rural Housing Alliance's
(RHA) information sheet on "How to Determine Interest Credit on
FmHA Loans.")

Families that qualify for interest credit homes may build their
homes by the self-help method if a self-help housing project is organized
or already operating in their community. Under the self-help system,
the families provide most of the labor required in building their homes
and thus reduce the cost of their individual loans by $3,000 or more.
The average self-help group consists of six to twelve families and requires about eight to ten months in construction time. Families that
use the self-help method save the labor cost—approximately 30 percent of the total cost—and also receive assistance from FmHA on pre-
paying the interest on their loans during the construction process.
(For more detailed information on self-help housing and the availability
of grant funds to cover the operating expenses of such projects, contact the Rural Housing Alliance.)

Self-Help Housing Technical Assistance
Grants (Section 523)

Section 523 self-help housing technical assistance grant funds
cover the operating costs of some 50 self-help housing nonprofit organizations throughout the United States, which are assisting approximately 1,500 families annually to build new homes. Congress appropriated about $6 million for this program in fiscal year 1975.

Its purpose is to provide organizations with the financial assistance necessary to pay the costs of developing, administering, or co-
ordinating programs of technical and supervisory assistance that will
aid low-income families in carrying out self-help housing efforts in
rural areas. Funds may be used to hire personnel; pay office expenses;

purchase office supplies; pay workmen's compensation, liability insurance, the employer's share of social security, travel, and training; purchase and rent power tools; and pay for training or for technical and consultant services.

The initial grant may not generally exceed $100,000 annually,
unless authorized by the national office, and covers a period of no
more than two years. No security is required, and those who may
qualify are public bodies and nonprofit corporations.

If the applicant is a private, nonprofit corporation, it should be
organized for the primary purpose of assisting low- and moderate-
income families to obtain adequate housing and have local representation among its membership. If the applicant lacks the proven ability to
perform responsibly in the field of self-help and cannot show proof of
other business management or administrative ventures, it must be
sponsored by an organization that has such a background. (For further information see FmHA Instruction 444.10 or contact RHA.)

Rental Housing Loans

Until recently, the rental housing loan program was utilized primarily for providing low-cost rental housing to senior citizens in rural
areas. More recently, however, this program has been substantially
expanded and the regulations revised so that it has the flexibility of
meeting the housing needs of other low-income families. In fiscal
year 1975, Congress made available approximately $300 million, of
which about $200 million was utilized for subsidized (interest credit)
loans for nonprofit housing developments.

The purpose of such loans may be any of the following: to construct, purchase, improve, alter, or repair rental housing, including
such related facilities as community rooms or buildings, cafeterias,
dining halls, recreation facilities, small garden plots, infirmaries,
assembly halls, central heating, sewage, light systems, ranges and
refrigerators, clothes-washing machines and dryers, and a safe domestic water system; purchase and develop housing sites, including
landscaping, foundation planting, seeding or sodding of lawns, development of walks, yards, fences, parking areas, and driveways; provide
office and living quarters of the resident manager and other operating
personnel; and pay fees for legal, architectural, engineering, and
other appropriate technical and official services. A nonprofit corporation or consumer cooperative may use loan funds to pay a qualified
consulting organization or foundation operating on a nonprofit basis
charges for necessary services.

The interest rate is 8.125 percent. Interest on loans to nonprofit
corporations and cooperatives providing housing for lower-income

families can be reduced to 1 percent with interest credits. Loans are repayable over 50 years, and there is no loan limit. Loans must be secured by a mortgage, and those who may qualify are individuals, nonprofit corporations, consumer cooperatives, profit-making corporations, and public bodies.

Public and private nonprofit organizations can operate on a county or regional basis and should have a substantial number of members in each community in which they plan to build rental housing. Maximum income levels of project occupants vary by state, but there are no income limits for senior citizen projects. Loans up to 102 percent may be available to nonprofit organizations in order to provide them with funds for initial operating costs. Occupants pay 25 percent of adjusted income, or 20 percent of adjusted income if utilities are not included in the rental charge. (For further information see FmHA Instruction 444.5, or write RHA for Informational Paper "Rental Housing Through the Farmers Home Administration.")

Rent Supplements

Under the 1974 housing act, FmHA was authorized to provide rent supplements to occupants of FmHA-financed rural rental housing projects to assist lower-income families that are currently ineligible due to inadequate income and lower-income families that are currently occupying rental units by paying more than 25 percent of their adjusted income. This program is the equivalent of the FHA's rent supplement program, which is utilized in conjunction with rental projects built under Section 236 of the 1968 Housing Act. This program in effect allows FmHA to serve many of the families it has in the past declared as ineligible for its services due to inadequate income.

HUD Section 8 Program

Section 8 of the housing act of 1974 is a new housing assistance program for lower-income families. This program is basically meant to replace all other subsidized housing programs under HUD and is a replacement specifically of the HUD Section 23 leased housing program A more detailed description of Section 8 was provided in the preceding chapter.

The importance of Section 8 to rural areas and small towns (whic receive a minimum of 20 percent and a maximum of 25 percent of the total units available each year) is potentially significant in that it theoretically will allow for the development of housing to serve more lower income families than FmHA is currently reaching through its interest credit rental program.

Under the Section 8 program, HUD agrees to help low-income families rent decent homes by helping them pay their rent. HUD will make up the difference between the approved rent for the unit and the amount the family pays (which is 15 to 25 percent of the family's adjusted income).

Units rented under Section 8 may be owned by private owners, both profit-making and nonprofit, and by public housing agencies. These units can be those financed under FmHA's Section 515 program. Although combining Section 8 and 515 appears feasible, and FmHA and HUD have issued written instructions as to how these programs are to be combined, there are several major problems that may create serious roadblocks and prevent the utilization of Section 8 with Section 515. First and foremost is FmHA's requirement that if any units in a Section 515 project are to receive Section 8 assistance payments, then the owner must not only provide evidence (through a market survey) that there is a sufficient number of eligible families in the area to fill these designated units, but he must also provide evidence that there would be a future market for these units without Section 8 assistance. In many cases in very poor communities, it will be difficult to find families that can afford to pay the full rent.

The second major obstacle is that HUD will not guarantee Section 8 assistance for projects financed by FmHA for more than 20 years, as opposed to the 40 years allowed for projects financed by state or local agencies. This in turn is causing FmHA to be overly cautious about using its funds for financing such projects, since FmHA loans are for 40 years. (For further information see FmHA Bulletin No. 5335 [444] or write RHA for its Information Paper "Rural Rental Housing and Section 8.")

Farm Labor Housing Loans and
Grants (Sections 514 and 516)

The farm labor housing combination loan and grant program is currently the only means of meeting the rental housing needs of low-income migrant and seasonal farmworkers (who are generally ineligible for other housing programs). Although the executive branch has been attempting to delete this program from its budget over the past few years, Congress continues to support it and provided some $15 million in fiscal year 1975.

These funds may be used for any of the following purposes: to construct or repair housing for farm laborers suitable for use on a year-round basis; improve the land on which the housing will be located by landscaping, foundation plantings, seeding and sodding lawns, construction of walks, yard fences, parking areas, and driveways; develop related facilities, such as community rooms or buildings, cafeterias, dining halls, infirmaries, child-care centers, assembly halls, central heating, sewage, lighting systems, bathing facilities, laundry facilities, and a safe domestic water supply; pay fees and charges for legal, architectural and other appropriate technical services; pay interest that will accrue on the loan from the date of loan closing to the estimated date of completion of construction; and provide household furnishings.

These loans bear an interest rate of 1 percent and are repayable over periods of up to 33 years. Grants may not exceed 90 percent of the cost of construction, and loans must be secured by a mortgage. Grants and loans may be made to nonprofit organizations of farmworkers, other nonprofit organizations, and public bodies. Nonprofit organizations can operate on a state-wide basis. Loans can also be made to farm owners. (For further information see FmHA Instruction 444.4 and 444.6; also see Code of Federal Regulations at 7 CFR 1822.61 through 1822.77 and 1822.201 through 1822.222.)

Loans for Home Repair (Section 504)

The Section 504 home repair loan program is aimed primarily at senior citizen homeowners who need to make minor repairs on their dwellings and are not eligible for a Section 502 loan. Congress has consistently appropriated $10-20 million annually for this program, which has proved to be very useful, although not widely utilized because of FmHA's reluctance to promote it in many areas. In those areas with Community Service Administration (OEO) and/or Department of Labor home repair projects, the Section 504 program has done much to improve local housing conditions, particularly for low-income senior citizens.

These loans may be used to make minor repairs and improvements to dwellings to make them safe and remove hazards to the health and safety of the owner, occupants, and community. Funds may be used to repair roofs, supply screens, repair structural supports, provide a convenient and sanitary water supply, provide toilet facilities, add a room to existing dwellings, and other similar repairs and improvements. This program may not be used for the construction of a new dwelling.

Loans of not more than $1,500 may be amortized over a period not to exceed 10 years; loans of $1,500 to $2,500 are for a maximum of 15 years; and loans of $2,500 to $5,000 are for a maximum of 20 years. The interest rate is 1 percent for all loans.

Those who may qualify include rural homeowners or lessees of housing sites who lack sufficient income to qualify for a Section 502 loan. Title to the property is not necessary if the applicant has evidence, such as tax payments, to prove he is considered by the community to be the owner. (For further information see FmHA Instruction 444.3 or write RHA for Information Paper on home repair loans.)

Rural Housing Site Loans
(Sections 523 and 524)

The Sections 523 and 524 rural housing site loans are to be used to purchase and develop adequate housing sites, including the construction of essential access roads, streets, utility lines, water and sewer systems; pay engineering fees, legal fees, closing costs, and incidental administrative expenses; provide landscaping, planting, seeding, sodding, walks, parking areas, driveways; and pay estimated interest that the applicant cannot pay from other sources.

The interest rate is 8.125, except for self-help housing sites, for which it is 3 percent. Payments on the loan are made as sites are sold. The final payment is due in two years. Normally, the borrower cannot owe more than $100,000. The loan must be secured by a mortgage, and both private and public nonprofit organizations may qualify.

If the nonprofit organization is not a public body, it must have a membership of at least 10 community leaders. Sites may be sold only to families having a low or moderate income that qualify for a Section 502 loan or to nonprofit organizations eligible for an FmHA rental or coop housing loan. If public water and waste disposal facilities are provided on a community basis, with funds included in the loan or other financing, provision should be made to form an organization that will provide continuing maintenance and management of facilities. (For further information see FmHA Instruction 444.8; also see Code of Federal Regulations 7 CFR 1822.261 through 1822.278.)

FmHA AND HOW IT OPERATES

Of the 1,700 county offices established by FmHA to serve all rural areas in the United States, most are located in the county seat town, with some offices serving several counties. In some cases, suboffices are maintained, at which the FmHA county supervisor will work only a few days each month.

There are several ways to locate the FmHA office that serves a specific rural area. Local offices are listed in the telephone book under "U.S. government, Department of Agriculture, Farmers Home Administration." The national FmHA office can also provide the correct address of your local FmHA office. Write the FmHA, Department of Agriculture, Washington, D.C. 20250. Or you can call or write the appropriate state FmHA director listed in Appendix E.

All applications for FmHA loans are made at the local county office. If you encounter any difficulty in working with a county office employee, you can appeal to the state director and, if necessary, write the Administrator, Farmers Home Administration, Washington, D.C. 20250. If you are still unsatisfied with the results of your appeal, write the Rural Housing Alliance, 1346 Connecticut Avenue, N.W., Washington, D.C. 20036.

FmHA instructions and procedures on their various housing programs can be purchased at minimal cost by writing to Management Information Systems Staff, Farmers Home Administration, USDA, South Building, Washington, D.C. 20250.

FINANCIAL AND TECHNICAL ASSISTANCE RESOURCES

For local church groups and others interested in improving housing conditions for low-income families and individuals in their communities, there are several avenues of approach. First and foremost, especially for groups with no prior experience in housing development, it is essential to determine what the local and regional organizations, both public and private, are doing about the housing problem in your area. There are several organizations that should be covered in your review.

Meeting with local, county, or regional housing authorities will provide you with a good indication of how your local public officials have responded to the housing need and, based on the number of families on the waiting list for housing units, what will be needed in the future. In many cases, the local Community Action Agency (CAP) serves as a nonprofit housing development agency or has established a separate nonprofit organization for this purpose and will be able to provide you with detailed information on the extent of the housing problem, what is being done about it, and how your group can become involved.

In many areas, the Council of Governments (COG) and local and regional planning commissions have received HUD Section 701 planning grant funds and are responsible for carrying out surveys and compiling information on the housing conditions and needs of local communities. In addition, these agencies in some cases have established nonprofit organizations to stimulate and sponsor low-income housing development projects. And, finally, in many areas throughout the United States, there are experienced, ongoing nonprofit housing organizations supported with grant funds from the Community Services Administration, Department of Labor, FmHA, Revenue Sharing, and other state and federal programs. These organizations, some relatively new and others with several years of experience, are a valuable source of information regarding housing needs and how local groups can join with them in helping to meet this need.

For local groups interested in establishing a nonprofit housing organization and becoming directly involved in low-income housing development, rental, home repair, homeownership, or a combination of these programs, there are several sources of financial and technical assistance resources available.

In most states there is a special branch, division, or agency within the state government that has at least a skeleton staff to research and publish information on state housing problems and needs and to provide basic technical and training assistance to public and private housing developers. In many states, this special staff is a part of the state Department of Housing and Community Affairs or the state Department of Commerce. In others, the state housing agency is a separate entity established by the state legislature with broad authorities to engage in a variety of housing development and finance activities.

The types of activity in which these state housing agencies engage and the direct assistance they can provide varies from state to state. Some agencies are authorized to provide only technical assistance and advice to local groups and may not be very aggressive in carrying out this limited service, particularly to rural organizations. Other states, however, have agencies that are authorized to (1) make seed-money loans (interest free in some cases) to nonprofit and other organizations for land option costs, architectural and engineering fees, and other initial expenses; (2) make loans for land acquisition and development costs; (3) provide direct loans for construction and permanent financing to developers of low-income housing; (4) serve as a secondary mortgage market to assist other financial institutions engaged in housing finance; and (5) undertake a variety of other educational and technical activities. And, perhaps most important, state housing agencies are to play a major role in the allocation and development of low-income housing under Section 8 of the 1974 housing act. In almost all states, the state housing agency will receive an allocation of the total amount of Section 8 funds designated for the state and will be responsible for allocating a portion of these funds to rural areas.

In summary, state housing agencies have many resources and services that can and should be utilized to the fullest extent by local nonprofit organizations.

In addition to state and federal housing agencies, there are three national nonprofit rural housing organizations that exist primarily to provide assistance to local groups and organizations involved in low-income housing development, to carry on research and educational activities, and to generally serve as advocates for improving housing opportunities for low-income rural Americans. These organizations provide a variety of services and information that can and should be utilized by local groups whenever needed.

RHA is the oldest, and was for several years the only, national rural housing organization in the United States. Founded in 1967 with the help of the American Friends Service Committee and supported by the Ford Foundation, RHA serves as a clearinghouse for information on rural housing; conducts research on rural housing needs and the response of the government to the rural housing problem; publishes informational and technical handbooks and materials on HUD and FmHA housing programs; serves as ombudsman for local groups frustrated in their dealings with public agencies; provides technical and financial assistance to organizations that plan, develop, and build houses for farmworkers and other low-income rural people; conducts rural housing conferences and workshops; and administers a $750,000 revolving loan fund available to local organizations for optioning, acquiring, and developing building sites for low-income housing. RHA is currently supported by membership contributions, a Department of Labor Migrant Division grant, and private donations. (For more information, write the Rural Housing Alliance, 1346 Connecticut Avenue, N.W., Washington, D.C. 20036.)

The National Rural Housing Coalition (NRHC) is a nonprofit, nonpartisan, public interest lobby organization, financed wholly by dues and gifts from members and other organizations. Founded in 1969 as an outgrowth of the First National Rural Housing Conference, NRHC is a full-time lobby operation devoted to improving rural housing programs and legislation to meet the housing needs of rural people. NRHC publishes a weekly newsletter on legislative activities related to rural housing. (For more information, contact the National Rural Housing Coalition, 1346 Connecticut Avenue, N.W., Washington, D.C. 20036.)

The Housing Assistance Council (HAC) is a national nonprofit housing organization established in 1971 by the OEO to provide training, technical assistance, research, educational materials, and predevelopment loans to improve rural housing throughout the United States. In addition to its work with local nonprofit organizations, HAC attempts to provide special assistance to public housing authorities and state housing agencies. (For more information, write the Housing Assistance Council, 1601 Connecticut Avenue, N.W., Washington, D.C. 20009.)

SERVICING THE PROJECT

Management and Human Relations

Servicing the project is a combination of operating a business and human relations. It is a business. Nonprofit housing organizations come into the housing field from the perspective of the "helping professions." This is a strength. Because business training and skills are not dominant in many nonprofit housing organizations, special care is appropriate. Bad business practices make for bad housing, and bad housing is worse than no housing because it can bankrupt the organization.

It is good business to know and use budgeting, good accounting methods, and good office procedures; keep the property looking good, provide good maintenance, and answer service calls promptly and competently; and screen applicants for housing carefully and thoroughly, expect prompt rent collection, and service people cheerfully.

Management is human relations. We house people. That is our business. When we house people we also house their problems. Dealing with residents requires managers to be in charge of their own lives and feelings. When we expect responsible behavior, it is more likely to be forthcoming.

A manager should be able to get in touch with his own feelings and those of others, especially those of the residents, and act on them appropriately. His philosophy of housing, policies, and conditions of the lease must be communicated, understood, and acted upon by all parties. He must be firm and evenhanded, and must treat the residents with dignity and respect. He should encourage and cooperate with resident organizations, be equipped to refer residents to the appropriate human resources, and keep residents informed as to the budget, costs, and the general well-being of the housing corporation.

Management Training

Housing management is becoming more of an industry. IREM has comprehensive courses for property management, which were described in detail in Chapter 6. The term "property manager" refers to the professional who usually has several properties and supervises resident managers. A Certified Property Manager has been certified by IREM upon completion of a required number of courses, had three years' experience, and has been observed to be reliable and competent.

The resident manager deals with one property and often lives on the property. He deals with the day-to-day operation of the project and is closest to the residents.

In nonprofit housing, the manager is usually a combination property manager and resident manager. He is hired by the corporation to service the project.

IREM has courses for resident managers conducted by its various local chapters. The Apartment Builders and Owners Councils under the National Association of Home Builders also has a training program. Some community colleges and several universities, such as Temple, have degree courses in management.

Since your project will most likely come under HUD regulations, you will visit your area HUD office and ask for the director of management. He will give you the name of the person with whom you will be working. New programs will be initiated under Section 8. The best source at present for guidelines on Section 8 is to read the Federal Register. The following HUD publications may be helpful:

HM G 4351.1 Insured Project Management Guide
HM G 7460.3 Housing for the Elderly
A Training Model for Low Rent Housing Management
Curriculum and Training Techniques for the Training of Para-
    professional Employees of Public Housing Authorities

There are many other HUD publications for all sorts of management situations. Your area office will help you secure what you need.

The following books published by IREM should also be helpful:

Principles of Real Estate Management, by James C. Downs, Jr.
The Resident Manager, by William Brauer
The Property Management Process, by Lloyd D. Handord, Sr.

Finally, visit some well-managed properties. This can be really beneficial. And remember that management training is a never-ending process. You will always continue to learn more about being better able to deliver quality housing.

The Management Plan

The management plan is a statement that is written and continued throughout the life of the project. It begins before anything else. After the original inspection, consultations, and, most likely, feasibility study are made by a reputable management consultation firm, you will put your management plan on paper. These are some of the subjects that must be covered:

1. What values led your organization into the field of housing?

2. What style of management do you propose? To hire a management company to manage for you, have residents do much of the management, do it yourself, or a combination of these?

3. Who is to be housed?

4. Why is this housing necessary?

5. Where is this housing to be built?

6. Everything that happens before real estate is purchased until occupancy: zoning and land use, financing (construction and long-term), choosing an architect, beauty of design, economy of design (maintenance-free, durable, low-cost construction), and attractive buildings and grounds.

Much of this has already been covered earlier in this Action Guide. It is important to begin servicing the project before the project development begins.

The Manager's Overall Responsibility

The actual needs and duties of management will vary greatly depending upon the location, size, and type of project. There are three broad areas of responsibility: marketing and public relations, operating the business, and operating the buildings. Each of these broad areas of responsibility has many facets and variations that will change from one development to another. We do not presume to deal with everything here. Rather, we will look at the multifamily housing field as practiced by nonprofit organizations.

Marketing the product has three distinct purposes: to get qualified prospects to the building, convince them that it is a good place to live, and keep existing residents satisfied with good management. That is right out of a textbook. But since you are in the low- and moderate-income housing field, money is a real problem. Some of the applicants come having cheated their previous or present landlord and are now setting you up for the same kind of treatment. At the same time, low-income people do not have many options for housing open to them.

You must know your housing philosophy, your management plan, and your feelings. Now you are ready to explore the seven steps of marketing.

Step one is to qualify the prospect. Government regulations require a certain space. If you have a HUD-insured project, you have all sorts of other requirements. Find out what they are and rough-screen first thing. Points of qualifying include race, sex, number, income, age, and eligibility.

Step two is to know your product. Know the good and the bad about your building—its privacy, security, and location. Be able to give information on transportation, recreational facilities, religious services, educational opportunities, shopping, employment, and community services.

Step three is to know your competition—the good and the bad.

Step four is product preparation. Have the buildings ready to rent at all times. Be neat, clean, and attractive yourself, and keep the vacant apartments the same way.

Step five is processing the rental. After getting a verbal agreement to rent, you enter into a new phase of activity. While you are really continuing your public relations function, you are also becoming involved with some detailed and technical procedures important to the success of your project: complete the lease application and the credit report; collect the security deposit; and verify income, eligibility, credit, and desirability.

Step six is resident orientation. State clearly and in writing management's expectations of the resident and also what the resident may expect of management. Communicate your housing philosophy.

Step seven is to welcome the occupancy. Welcome them to a clean, well-repaired apartment.

Marketing and public relations do not end with a signed lease. They are ongoing processes in which community spirit prevails.

Operating the Business

A well-run business brings you halfway home. Without that, the venture is crippled.

The operating budget includes only those cash items of income and expense that are anticipated during that particular budget year. Government regulation requires that reserves be built to provide for replacement, unforeseen emergencies, and obsolescence. These funds are set aside and are not a part of the operating budget. Figure 6 shows a sample operating budget.

A stabilized budget is a forecast of income and expenses that can be supported and represents an average projected over a foreseeable number of years. This statement begins where the annual operating budget ends and goes on into the future. Accordingly, the following assumptions are made in today's market: the rate of inflation; the current trend of rising real estate taxes plus other levies against property; increased projected labor costs; projected annual income for the foreseeable future; insurance cost increases; increased costs for contract services, such as gardening, elevator maintenance, rubbish and snow removal, and pest control; and rising costs for materials, supplies, and administration. Figure 7 shows a sample five-year stabilized budget.

Additional income can be expected from parking, franchises, tenant-charged utilities, vending and laundry machines, tenant-charged special services, signs, and the sale of utilities and services to other properties.

There is a myth in the housing industry that nonprofit organizations are soft on rent collections. This is not true. Any corporation, for-profit or not, that is soft on rent collection will not be around for long. When rents are not conscientiously collected, it hurts those who pay. It is poor business and false economy to grant "welfare payments" to those who do not pay. Your nonprofit corporation cannot engage in that kind of giving. Collect every payment every time. The best time to deal with nonpayment is yesterday. Some residents pay regularly and responsibly; others have problems once in a while. Some are always late and in arears. Others are con artists and have perfected the rip-off. Finally, there are those who are experiencing hard times, such as illness or the loss of a job. Deal with this immediately. You do not need to get caught as rescuer, victim, or persecutor, as you do or do not collect the rent. Treat people with the expectation that they are responsible.

Operating the Building

The manager must be alert and responsive to calls residents make for service. There are certain guidelines that should be kept in mind. Do preventative maintenance to get at repair and replacement before a breakdown. While answering a service call in a residence, check on and perform other routine maintenance. When rents are paid or when you see your residents, ask how things are with the apartment. Encourage people to call you when they have problems that need attention. Answer service calls with dispatch and effectiveness.

A sense of community is achieved when residents see their self-interest served by keeping a project clean and in a cared-for state. They become part of the solution instead of part of the problem.

Resident Organizations

For quality management, resident organization is essential. For insensitive or incompetent management, resident organization is a threat. When considering resident organization, we immediately get into the area of ownership.

FIGURE 6

Sample Operating Budget
(in dollars)

	Latest Year		Budget Next Year
Income			
Current possible rental income	110,000	Possible income with 5 percent rent increase for 50 percent of space	112,750
Possible income from other sources	10,000	3 percent increase average 50 percent of year	10,150
Total possible income	120,000	Total possible income	122,900
Less latest year rent losses at 5 percent	6,000	Less probable 5 percent rent loss	7,374
Effective gross income	114,000	Budgeted gross effective income	115,526
Expenses			
Real estate taxes	15,000	4 percent increase for half-year	15,300
Gross salaries and other employee compensation	8,000	5 percent increase three-quarters of year	8,300
Utilities (each listed)	3,000	3 percent increase full year	3,090
Contract services	2,500	4 percent increase full year	2,600
Supplies (list by types)	400	5 percent increase full year	420
Repairs and replacements (minor)	1,000	5 percent increase full year	1,050
Repairs and replacements (major)	—	To be paid for during year (itemize)	5,000
Insurance (list by types)	600	5 percent increase full year	630
Management at 6 percent of effective gross	6,840	Management at 6 percent of budgeted effective gross	6,932
Legal, accounting, and other administrative	450	5 percent increase full year	473
Net operating income	76,210	Net operating income	71,731
To balance	114,000	To balance	115,526

If the property is encumbered with mortgage loan financing, the following budget addendum is included:

	Latest Year		Budget Next Year
Net operating income	76,210	Net operating income	71,731
Less interest on financing	31,018	Less interest on financing	29,518
Subtotal	45,192	Subtotal	42,204
Less paid A/C loan principal	15,500	Less paid A/C loan principal	17,000
Cash flow	29,692	Cash flow	25,204
Cash flow reduced to reflect monthly income to ownership: 2,482		Cash flow reduced to reflect monthly income to ownership: 2,100	

Source: Lloyd D. Henford, Sr., Property Management Process (Chicago: Institute of Real Estate Management, 1972), p. 5.

FIGURE 7

Sample Five-Year Stabilized Budget
(in dollars)

	Base Year	Stabilized
Total Possible Income		
Gross space rentals	100,000	101,200
Other income (itemize)	8,000	8,200
Total gross income	108,000	109,400
Less rent losses	3,200	3,700
Effective gross income	104,800	105,700
Expenses		
Real estate taxes and licenses	15,000	16,249
Gross salaries, taxes, and fringe	8,000	8,666
Utilities (itemize)	4,000	4,081
Contract services (itemize)	3,000	3,250
Supplies (itemize)	400	433
Minor repairs and replacements (itemize)	900	975
Ordinary painting and decorating	500	542
Insurance (itemize)	600	624
Management	4,200	4,435
Legal and accounting	350	375
Roof replacement*	—	1,000
Carpet replacement*	—	1,500
Boiler rehabilitation*	—	600
Other major expenditures* (itemize)	—	1,000
Total expenses	36,950	43,730
Net operating income	68,850	61,970
To balance	105,800	105,700

*These are total costs allocated on an annual basis over the five-year projection period. In calculating total costs, adjustments should be made from present estimates to reflect probable costs at the time the work will be contracted for.

Source: Lloyd D. Henford, Sr., Property Management Process (Chicago: Institute of Real Estate Management, 1972), p. 10.

It is a truism that people who own a building will be inclined to better care for it than if they rent. There are various levels of ownership in multifamily housing.

Condominiums and cooperatives are when various persons, usually the occupants, own a part of the whole. They own the cubic footage and have a voice in the affiars of the corporation that owns the land, walls, floor, and so on. Not many low- or middle-income people can afford this investment.

Ownership of "turf" is more of a frame of mind than anything else. In garden apartments, each resident may have some back or front yard for which he is responsible. Management and neighbors respect this turf as much as the inside of the apartments. This process is enhanced when the resident is given paint, repair materials, and training for self-improvement of the unit.

Ownership of management refers to the process by which the resident has a voice in the management of the property. Through the democratic process, representatives can be elected to councils to help in the areas of maintenance policy; beauty, safety, and cleanliness of the property; rent increases; garbage and trash handling; screening of new residents; pet policy; and the general well-being of the community. Outright ownership of equity may not be possible. But having a piece of the action and owning at least some of the management of property in which a person lives helps dignify a resident. This kind of ownership will reduce the resident turnover, vandalism, property damage, and so on.

When resident organizations do not function very well, it is usually because there is no issue apparent or open to the residents or there is no hope for the resident to be able to use his power to control his own destiny.

Special features, such as food coops, homemaking demonstrations, and community landscaping, may be useful amenities. Often governmental agencies will work cooperatively with management to better deliver human services. Office or meeting space might be given for outside personnel to use for the well-being of the residents.

GLOSSARY OF TERMS

General Terminology

Adjusted Income

What remains of recurring income after subracting 5 percent for payroll deductions and $300 per minor child or dependent. The government uses a percentage of the adjusted income (20 to 25 percent) in a number of programs to determine how much subsidy a family or an individual should receive in housing and how much the family or individual must pay.

Condemnation

An action taken by the local, state, or federal government to prohibit the continued use of property. Condemnation proceedings are initiated for two reasons:

Public safety: This action is taken when the continued use of the property presents a public health hazard or is dangerous. Under this proceeding, the owner of the property is not compensated for the loss of the property.
Public use: This action, also called an "Eminent Domain" proceeding, is taken when a property is needed for a public purpose, such as the construction of schools or roads. Under this proceeding, the courts determine the fair market value and the owner is paid for the property.

Debt Service

Payments made on loans, which include interest charges and a portion of the principal sum borrowed. Debt service payments may also include amounts to be placed in escrow accounts for payment of tax and/or insurance costs when due.

Depreciation

The decrease in value of property as a result of use. For tax purposes, the estimated depreciation on an income-producing property's value can offset the taxes due on the income produced by the property. In real estate, this tax benefit is available to the owners of the property, but not to tenants or homeowners.

Accelerated Depreciation. This is a means through which the government allows the owner of income-producing property to depreciate its value rapidly and unrelated to its real worth on the open market. For example, a rental unit with an anticipated useful life of 20 years can be depreciated to nothing in 10 years, thus allowing the owner greater reductions for those 10 years in taxes paid on income. Accelerated depreciation on rental property can be taken each time ownership of the property changes. This device was designed to generate and encourage investment as a stimulus to the economy.

Docket

The complete packet of documents required before a loan can be closed.

Down Payment

An initial amount of money paid by the purchaser to the seller of the house. The amount of money required for down payments generally depends on the availability of mortgage credit. When the amount of available mortgage money is great, mortgage financers will require less in down payment. When mortgage credit is tight, mortgage financers will require more in down payment. With FmHA financing, down payments are usually not required. With FHA insurance, some down payment is generally required.

Dwelling Unit

An apartment unit, regardless of type and size, or a single-family house.

Feasibility Study

The process by which projected costs, income from rents, and the prospective tenants' ability to pay are measured against each other to see whether a rental project will be economically possible.

Federal Housing Administration (FHA)

An agency of HUD that provides mortgage insurance for single- and multifamily housing and can provide subsidies for low-income housing.

FHA Loans

Loans made by private lenders and insured by FHA.

Fire and Hazard Insurance

Insurance covering loss or damage to property caused by fire and/or natural disasters, such as tornadoes and hurricanes.

Farmers Home Administration (FmHA)

An agency of the Department of Agriculture that administers housing and other programs for rural areas and small towns.

FmHA Loans

Loans made by the FmHA directly to the borrower from funds provided by congressional appropriations or, more commonly, from a revolving fund that is replenished by selling mortgages on loans made on the open market.

Housing

Cooperative Housing. Units that are owned by an incorporated, democratically controlled organization composed of the occupants. Management of cooperative housing can be provided by the cooperative itself or by a management corporation under contract to the cooperative.

Housing Development Corporation. A multipurpose, generally non-profit, private housing corporation established to serve a given geographic area—a neighborhood, city, state, or region—by providing technical assistance, lending seed money, and directly sponsoring housing developments.

Dilapidated Housing. Usually refers to the Census Bureau's definition of housing that cannot be made habitable even with major rehabilitation.

Existing Housing. Occupied or unoccupied housing units.

Federally Assisted Housing. Housing that has been financed with assistance provided by one of the federal housing agencies. The assistance may be through the provision of FHA mortgage insurance, reduction of interest to the borrower, the payment of capital and operating costs through public housing, and so on.

Housing Goals. The estimate by the government of the amount of unassisted and assisted housing units that need to be produced between
1968 and 1978 to adequately house all Americans. The official goals
were considered to be underestimates by two presidential commissions
and a number of organizations deeply concerned about housing, and
the goals for yearly production needed to meet the overall goals have
yet to be met.

Limited Dividend Corporation. A profit-motivated housing development sponsor, which can earn up to 6 percent profit annually on its
equity investment. Limited dividends provide a device for investors
to make profits while benefiting from accelerated depreciation (tax
write-offs).

Nonprofit Housing. Any housing constructed or developed from which
the owner is not supposed to make a profit.

Nonprofit Housing Corporation. A legally incorporated organization
which may, depending on its purposes, develop, own, sponsor, or
manage housing at no profit to itself.

Open Housing. A result of the passage of the 1964 Civil Rights Act,
which forbids discrimination in housing on the basis of race or creed.

Overcrowded Housing. According to the Census Bureau, any unit that
has more than 1.01 persons per room, excluding kitchens and bathrooms.

Public Housing. A HUD program that provides the greatest subsidies
to low-income people. It pays for the entire capital costs (land, development, and construction) and can pay some of the maintenance
and management costs. Tenants in public housing pay no more than
25 percent of their adjusted incomes in rent (there are homeownership
as well as rental programs). Public housing can be established in an
area only with the approval of a local unit of government.

Substandard Housing. Either dilapidated or lacking essential plumbing facilities (hot or cold running water, flush toilet, and tub or shower)
for the exclusive use of residents of the unit.

Department of Housing and Urban Development (HUD)

The cabinet department that administers a number of programs, including FHA, Model Cities, Public Housing, Urban Renewal, and Operation Breakthrough.

Interest Rate

Interest is the "rent" paid for borrowed money. It is the percentage of the sum borrowed that the borrower must pay each year to the lender for the use of the borrowed money.

Judgment

A court action that decrees that a lender can secure satisfaction on a debt through appropriation of the debtor's property. Except under extraordinary circumstances, it is unlikely that a lender will make a housing loan to anyone with a judgment against him.

Land Speculation

The practice of investing in land with the expectation that its value will increase in the future. Its practice is common in rapidly expanding metropolitan areas. Land speculation is a significant factor contributing to the rapid increase in land prices and therefore the cost of housing.

Land Write-Down

The procedure whereby a government agency disposes of the land for less than the price that the agency paid to acquire it. It is usually associated with urban renewal.

Lease

A contract for the possession of land or housing at stipulated compensation for a specified length of time.

Leasehold

Possession of property through a lease agreement, as contrasted to freehold, or ownership.

Lien

A financial claim on property.

Loan, Conventional

A loan made by a private source of credit, such as a bank or savings and loan association, without government insurance.

Loan, Direct

A loan made by the government directly to the borrower.

Loan, Insured

In the case of FHA, a loan made by a private lender and insured by the government. In the case of FmHA, a loan made from its revolving loan fund, which is replenished by insuring mortgages and selling them on the open market.

Maintenance Costs

The amount of money an occupant pays to maintain a dwelling in decent repair, including roof, window glass, paint, plumbing, replacement of hot water tanks, and so on.

Management Costs

The amount of money an occupant, generally a renter, pays for bookkeeping, staff (including janitorial), salaries, and so on.

Market Survey

A study that determines whether there are enough potential tenants in an area to justify a public housing or rental project. The study measures the availability, cost, and condition of existing housing against the potential tenants' ability to pay projected rentals.

Multifamily Development

A development of more than two dwellings or units, usually associated with garden apartments, townhouses, and high-rises.

Packager

A person or organization that acts on behalf of an individual, profit or nonprofit organization, or local housing authority on the initial processing, financing, and development of a housing project for a consultative fee.

Rehabilitation

The process by which substandard housing is made decent, safe, and sanitary by replacing the floors, roofs, bathrooms, kitchens, wiring, and so on.

Rent, Basic

The minimum rent that must be charged to cover all costs, including maintenance, management, and reserves, in a rental project and to repay the mortgage financing at 1 percent interest.

Rent, Market

The rent necessary to cover all costs, including maintenance, management, profit, and reserves, in a rental project and to repay the mortgage financing without any interest reduction.

Standard Metropolitan Statistical Area (SMSA)

A county or group of counties constituting an integrated economic and social unit, having at least one central city (or two adjoining cities that constitute a single community) with a population of 50,000 or more.

Sponsor

A public or private profit or nonprofit organization that accepts responsibility to maintain, manage, and pay for housing developed under its auspices.

Subsidy Mechanism

The method through which public or private agencies reduce the cost of housing to the homeowner or tenant. Examples of public subsidy mechanisms are the interest credit program available through FHA and FmHA and the use of manpower training resources in reducing labor costs. An example of a private subsidy mechanism is the purchase, development, and sale of land on a nonprofit basis.

Tax Abatement

A means through which a project is exempted by a unit of local government from local taxes or pays a reduced rate of taxes for a specified period of time. Abatements are often used to attract industries to a state or locality.

Tax Exemption

The permission granted by the government to certain individuals and organizations to not pay taxes on income and/or property. In real estate, for example, recognized churches are generally exempt from paying property taxes. Nonprofit housing corporations are exempt from paying federal income tax on receipts from rental units, although generally not from paying property taxes.

Property Tax

A compulsory payment to the government on real property. The amount is based on a percentage (as set by the government) of the assessed value (as assessed by the government) of the property. Property taxes usually bear a major portion of financing public services, such as school systems, on the local level.

Tax Write-off

A means by which property owners can make deductions from taxable income for depreciation, interest payments, or other taxes paid on property.

Turn-Key

A term used by housing contractors or developers to indicate that a dwelling is completed and ready for occupancy. It also refers to specific program options available through HUD's public housing program.

Veteran's Administration (VA)-Guaranteed Loan

A loan made to an eligible veteran by a private lender that is partially guaranteed (VA agrees to pay 60 percent of the loan in case of default by the veteran) by VA.

Building Terms

Code, Building

A set of regulations issued by a state or local government that establishes minimum requirements that must be met in the construction of buildings. Building codes cover both what materials can be used in construction and how the building must be constructed (minimum square footage, slope of roof, spacing of supports, height of building, height and width of windows and doorways, and so on). (Building codes sometimes have an exclusionary effect by requiring overbuilding and costly materials.)

Code, Health

A set of regulations issued and administered by the U.S. Public Health Department establishing minimum health standards that must be maintained to safeguard the health of a community. The local health department will determine, for instance, the lot size necessary for the installation of septic tanks, given the soil conditions.

Code, Housing

A set of regulations issued by a state or local government establishing the minimum conditions that must be fulfilled for the continued occupancy of a unit of housing. A housing code might require, for example, an electrical outlet for every four feet of wall space.

Code, Zoning

A set of regulations issued by a state or local government governing the use of land, for example, by establishing minimum lot sizes or determining which areas can be commercially developed. (Zoning codes sometimes have an exclusionary effect by making minimum lot sizes so large as to price land out of the range of many people.)

Contractor, General

An individual or corporation that provides certain goods or services under contract. Housing contractors are responsible for the construction of a dwelling unit in accordance with the terms set forth in the contract or other agreements.

Contractor, Sub-

A subcontractor is generally responsible for only a portion of the dwelling unit (he might only install the plumbing) and is responsible to the general contractor.

Easement

A legal agreement between the landowner and another party that gives access by the second party to the landowner's property for agreed

upon purposes. Easements are generally granted to public utility
companies, such as gas, electric, and telephone, for the provision of
services.

Housing

Borrower-Method. An approach that allows, with FmHA approval,
the borrower to be his own general contractor and to work on the construction of his house.

Industrialized. Factory-produced housing that can be assembled on
site to form a house or shipped as a completed unit. The parts produced in the factory may be panels, modules, or other component
parts. The term "component housing system" is sometimes used
synonymously with industrialized housing.

Mobile. Factory-built housing generally equipped with carpets and
furniture. The completed house can be shipped over the road to any
site. The term "trailer" is sometimes used synonymously with mobile homes.

Modular. Factory-built parts of the house (bath, kitchen, or individual rooms) that are shipped to a site for erection. They may consist
of two half-sections shipped on a trailer, which are then joined to
form a house.

Self-Help. A method of construction that allows low-income families
to realize significant cost reductions and accumulation of equity through
the pooling of their labor in groups of six to fourteen families. Mortgage financing generally is through FmHA's Section 502 loan.

Stick-Built. Housing built on site with no, or only minor, prefabrica-
tion of any parts. This is also called "conventional construction."

Inspector

A local government official who has the legal right to enforce
zoning, building, and housing codes within a given jurisdiction.

Percolation Test

A soil test required by local building and health departments to
determine the rate at which water is absorbed by the soil. It is usually
required when septic tanks are proposed for sewage disposal.

Septic Tank

A tank in which solid organic sewage is decomposed and purified by anaerobic bacteria. This system of sewage disposal is most frequently used in areas without adequate community sewage disposal facilities.

Specifications

Supplements to house plans and drawings that contain lists of details and products to be included in the building. They may be brief descriptions of materials or complete specifications listing the size, manufacturer, grade, color, style, and price of each item of material to be ordered.

Subdivision

A section of land that has been legally divided, usually by surveying and recording of plot at the county offices, into smaller building sites.

Survey

The process of ascertaining the location, form, and boundaries of a tract or area of land.

Workmen's Compensation

Insurance to protect an employee against injury or death resulting from his employment.

Real Estate/Financing Terms

Amortization

The process of repayment of a loan (debt reduction). Usually, housing loans are amortized by making equal monthly payments to the lender for the length of the mortgage period.

Appraisal

An estimate of the real, or market, value of a property; that is, what the owner could reasonably expect to get if he were to sell it. Appraisals are usually made by professional real estate appraisers, private or governmental.

Assessed Valuation

The value assigned to a piece of property by local government for real estate tax purposes. It is usually less than the market value of the property. The relationship between assessed value and market value varies from property to property and from jurisdiction to jurisdiction.

Capital

Capital Costs. The actual brick-and-mortar costs involved in the construction of a house, usually including land and development costs, materials, financing costs, labor, overhead, and profit. They do not include maintenance, reserve, administration, or operating costs. On a turn-key contract, the capital cost is the actual cost of the completed house paid to the builder.

Capital Investment. The value of actual cash or other goods exchanged for land or real property. For low-income buyers, their down payment or the value of self-help labor usually constitutes their capital investment.

Capital Requirements: The amount of money, usually 10 percent of capital costs, that profit-making or limited-dividend corporations must provide to be elibigle for participation in rental housing programs of FHA.

Closing

A meeting of the parties to a mortgage transaction or transfer of title to property. The documents necessary to accomplish these events are signed (executed) and delivered to the persons entitled to receive them, usually in the presence of lawyers to both parties.

Deed

A legal document that serves as evidence of ownership of real property.

Deed of Trust. An instrument in use in many states, taking the place and serving the purposes of a mortgage, by which legal title to real property is placed in one or more trustees, to secure the repayment of a sum of money or the performance of other conditions.

Quitclaim Deed. A deed provided to the buyer of property that indicates that the title is clear but does not guarantee it against outside
claims.

Warranty Deed. A deed that guarantees to the property buyer that the
title is free of liens and outside claims.

Equity

The value of an owner's interest in property in excess of outstanding claims or liens. For example, a homeowner's equity would
be the difference between the market value of the house and the amount
of the unpaid mortgage.

Financing Costs

The amount of interest the builder of housing will pay on the
money he borrows to purchase land, materials, and labor (see "Financing, Interim"). These costs are generally absorbed by the buyer
of the house in the purchase price.

Financing, Interim

A short-term loan covering the costs of land, building materials,
current real estate taxes, and other incidental expenses incurred during the construction period. An interim or construction loan is usually
obtained by the builder.

Financing, Permanent

A long-term loan, obtained by the buyer or owner, to cover the
capital costs of the dwelling. This is sometimes referred to as a
"take-out" loan.

FNMA/Fannie Mae

Federal National Mortgage Association. This was created by
the housing act of 1964 as a publicly owned corporation to buy and sell
mortgages in order to support the secondary mortgage market. Under
provisions of the 1968 housing act, FNMA is being converted to private
ownership. Those functions necessary to implement housing assistance efforts but impractical from the standpoint of private enterprise
are carried on by its sister agency, GNMA.

GNMA/Ginny Mae

Government National Mortgage Association. A public corporation established and operated by the government whose function is to provide a secondary market for mortgages on low-income housing programs. Through this, a flow of mortgage money for these programs from private sources is encouraged.

Land Contract

A contract for the purchase of real estate on an installment basis. Upon payment of the last installment, the deed is delivered to the buyer.

Market Interest Rate (MIR)

Generally, the maximum amount of interest that can be charged on federally insured mortgages. For FmHA loans, the rate is determined at the start of the fiscal year by the Treasury Department and is based on a formula geared to what it costs the government to borrow. For FHA-insured loans, the rate is set periodically by the secretary of HUD and is geared to the prevailing rates of interest charged on conventional mortgages.

Below-Market Interest Rate (BMIR). Applies to certain HUD-assisted programs in which the interest rate is subsidized by the federal government. For BMIR projects, the mortgage is purchased by the government from a private lending institution. Since 1968, this service has been performed by GNMA.

Mortgage

A lien placed against real property to secure a loan agreement between borrower and lender.

Mortgage, Second. A lien that is subordinated to a first mortgage and is used to secure a supplemental loan to the borrower.

Mortgage Insurance

A policy, usually taken on the head of the household, that will fulfill all mortgage commitments in the event he should become disabled or die.

Mortgage Market

The source of commercial credit for the purchase of mortgages. Usually refers to commercial investors, such as mortgage banks, insurance companies, and pension plans, which deal in loans for commercial or residential construction. Financing generally runs to large project mortgages as opposed to individual mortgages.

Mortgage Market, Secondary. The source of financing for the purchase of mortgages from the original lender. This device is utilized to increase the supply of credit available to the housing industry. FNMA will serve as a secondary market, for example, during periods when financing is tight by purchasing mortgages from private investors, thus freeing credit for additional investment in housing.

Mortgage Paper

The security that the lender holds on the loan made to the borrower. The lender, particularly FmHA, often sells the mortgage paper on the open market to private investors, guaranteeing that the mortgage will be paid off and guaranteeing a set return on the investment. Through this mechanism, the lender replenishes lending capital.

Mortgage Period

The length of time the borrower has to repay his housing loan. Mortgages generally have periods of at least 20 years. Mortgages under federally assisted programs are generally for 30 to 50 years.

Mortgage Terms

The conditions that the borrower must meet to fulfill his obligations.

Mortgagee

The person to whom the mortgage is given; that is, the lender.

Mortgagor

The person who mortgages his property, or the borrower.

Option

An acquired right, usually a written option agreement, to buy or sell property at a fixed price within a specified time.

Points

Charges made by a lending institution to increase its return or investment. Generally, one point is equal to 1 percent of the loan and represents an added cost to the borrower. They are usually associated with federally insured mortgages, which carry a ceiling on allowable interest charges, which may be less than what a lender can charge on other kinds of loans.

Principal

The outstanding balance of a loan. Mortgage payments are separated into two parts—one goes to pay interest on the loan and the other to reduce the principal.

Promissory Note

A written promise to repay a sum of money, specifying the terms and conditions of repayment.

Realtor

A real estate broker who is a member of the National Association of Real Estate Boards. He can be the official agent (or go-between) for either buyer or seller and receives a fee for services rendered.

Reamortization

A method to allow a delinquent borrower to pay off what he is behind by spreading this amount over the balance of the mortgage period, thereby making his payments higher. Since FmHA is prohibited in most circumstances from refinancing loans, this is a method used to avoid foreclosure on a borrower.

Refinancing

A method by which the original mortgage is paid off through issuing a new mortgage to either the original borrower or a new one. Refinancing is generally used either to extend the mortgage period or to achieve more favorable interest terms.

Security

The means by which the lender assures himself that his money is protected should the borrower default on the loan. The security on a car loan, for example, is generally the car itself. The security on housing loans is the housing, as secured by the mortgage.

Seed Money/Front Money

The amount of capital needed to get a project off the ground, usually recoverable in the mortgage loan. Items for which front money is usually needed are the option agreement, partial payment of professional services, site surveys, FHA fees, and FNMA fees.

Site

The land or property to be developed for new construction or rehabilitation.

Title

The legal sum of all evidence that constitutes a proof of ownership.

Title Insurance

An insurance policy that protects the holder of the title from claims against the property.

Title Search (Abstract)

A method of checking the condition of the title to a piece of property by examination of official records dealing with transactions involving the property.

Mortgage Terms

Abstract of Title

A written history of the title transaction or conditions that affect the title of a designated parcel of land from the original source of title to the present, consisting of a summary of all the instruments disclosed by the records setting forth their material parts.

Adverse Possession

The right of an occupant of land to acquire title against the real owner, where possession has been actual, continuous, hostile, visible, and distant for the statutory period.

Affidavit

A statement or declaration, reduced to writing and sworn or affirmed to before an officer who has the authority to administer an oath or affirmation.

Amortization

The gradual reduction of a debt by means of periodic payments sufficient to pay principal and thereby liquidate the debt.

Appraisal

The act of placing an estimate of value on real property and the process of preparing such an estimate.

Assessed Valuation

The valuation placed upon real or personal property for purposes of taxation.

Assessment

A charge made against property by the state, county, cities, and authorized districts.

Bankrupt

Any person, firm, or corporation unable to pay its debts and whose assets become liable to administration under bankruptcy law for the protection of its creditors.

Below-Market Interest Rate (BMIR)

Applies to certain HUD-assisted programs in which the interest rate is subsidized by the federal government. For BMIR projects, the mortgage is purchased by the government from a private lending institution. Since 1968, this service has been performed by GNMA.

Borrower

One who receives funds, with the expressed or implied intention
of repaying the loan in full or giving the equivalent.

Broker

One who, for a commission or fee, brings parties together and
assists in negotiating contracts between them. In real estate transactions, the broker usually brings together the buyer and the seller and
the mortgage lender.

Capital Investment

The value of actual cash or other goods exchanged for land or
real property. For low-income home buyers, their down payment or
the value of self-help labor usually constitutes their capital investment.

Capital Requirements

The amount of money that profit-making or limited-dividend
corporations must provide to be eligible for participation in federally
assisted housing programs.

Capital Costs

The actual brick-and-mortar costs involved in the construction
of a house, usually including land and development costs, materials,
labor, overhead, and profit. They do not include maintenance, reserve, administration, or operating costs. On a turn-key contract,
the capital cost is the actual cost of the completed house paid to the
builder.

Chain of Title

A succession of conveyance carried through to the last person,
usually commencing with a patent deed.

Chattel Mortgage

A mortgage on personal property.

Closing

A meeting of the parties to a mortgage transaction or transfer
of title to property. The documents necessary to accomplish these

events are signed (executed) and delivered to the persons entitled to receive them, usually in the presence of lawyers to both parties.

Cloud on Title

A proceeding or instrument, such as a deed, deed of trust, or mortgage, or a tax or assessment, a judgment, or decree, which, if valid, would impair the title of land.

Collateral

Stocks, bonds, evidence of deposit, and other marketable properties that a borrower pledges as security for a loan. In mortgage lending, the collateral is the specific real property that the borrower pledges as security.

Condemnation

The lawful taking of private property for public use. The owner must be given a fair price, and the property must be acquired only for some special need. The right of the state or its political subdivisions to condemn property is called "the right of eminent domain."

Construction Loan

A loan made by a private source of credit, such as a bank or savings and loan association, without government insurance.

Conveyance

The transfer of the title to land from one person or class of persons to another.

Covenant

An agreement between two or more persons, entered into by deed whereby one of the parties promises the performance or nonperforman of certain acts or that a given state of things does or shall, or does not or shall not, exist.

Deed

An instrument in writing, under seal and duly executed and delivered, containing a transfer, bargain, or contract, usually conveying the title to real property from one party to another. There are tw

types of deed—the quitclaim and the warranty. Under the quitclaim
deed, the seller conveys property to the purchaser, the title being
only as good as the title held by the seller, who conveys all claim, interest, or right to the property as far as his own title is concerned.
Under a warranty deed, the seller also conveys all claim, right, and
title to the property but in addition warrants the title to be clear subject only to such matters as may be shown in the deed. The warranty
is recognized by law as the subject for future restitution of loss to the
purchaser if any defects in the title are conveyed by the seller. A
seal is not required in some states, and the term "grant deed" is used
in place of "warranty deed" in some states.

Deed of Trust

A conveyance of the total land to a trustee as collateral security
for the payment of a debt with the condition that the trustee shall re-
convey the title upon the payment of the debt, and with power of the
trustee to sell the land and pay the debt in the event of a default on
the part of the debtor.

Deed Restrictions

Limitations placed in a deed limiting or restricting the use of
the land.

Demand Mortgage

A mortgage that is payable on demand by the holder of the evidence of the debt.

Direct Loan

A loan made by the government directly to the borrower.

Easement

A right or interest in the land of another that entitles the holder
thereof to some use, privilege, or benefit, such as to place pole lines,
pipeline, roads thereon, or to travel over.

Eminent Domain

The inherent right of a sovereign power to appropriate all or
any part of the private property within its borders for a necessary use
by the public, with or without the consent of the owner, by making reasonable payment to such owner.

Encroachment

An unlawful extension of one's right upon the land of another.

Encumbrance

A claim or lien upon an estate.

Equity

The value of an owner's interest in property in excess of out-standing claims or liens. For example, a homeowner's equity would be the difference between the market value of the house and the amount of the unpaid mortgage.

Escrow

Securities, instruments, or other property deposited by two or more persons with a third person, to be delivered on a certain contingency or the happening of a certain event; when used in the expression "in escrow," the state of being so held. The subject matter of the transaction is the escrow; the terms with which it is deposited with the third person constitute the escrow agreement; and the third person is the escrow agent.

Exceptions

Reflected in opinions, deeds, and title insurance.

Extended Coverage

Insurance agreed to and paid for by the insured, which covers fire, lightning, windstorm, hail, aircraft damage, vehicle damage, riot, explosion, and smoke damage.

FNMA/Fannie Mae

Federal National Mortgage Association. Created by the housing act of 1964 as a publicly owned corporation to buy and sell mortgages in order to support the secondary mortgage market. Under provisions of the 1968 housing act, FNMA is being converted to private owner-ship. Those functions necessary to implement housing assistance efforts but impractical from the standpoint of private enterprise are carried on by its sister agency, GNMA.

Fee, Simple

An absolute fee; a fee without limitation as to any restrictions or any particular class of heirs.

Fire Insurance

A contract whereby, for an agreed premium, one party undertakes to compensate the other for loss of a specific subject by reason of fire.

First Mortgage

A mortgage that is a first lien on the property pledged as security.

Foreclosure

The legal process by which a mortgagor of real or personal property or other owner of a property subject to a lien is deprived of his interest therein. The usual method is sale of the property either by court proceedings or outside of court.

GNMA/Ginny Mae

Government National Mortgage Association. A public corporation established and operated by the government whose function is to provide a secondary market for mortgages on low-income housing programs. Through this means, a flow of mortgage money from private sources for these programs is encouraged.

Hazard Insurance

A contract whereby for an agreed premium, one party undertakes to compensate the other for loss on a specific subject by specified hazards, such as acts of God or war.

Homestead Estate

The rights of record of the head of a family or household in real estate, owned and occupied as a home, which are exempt from seizure by creditors.

Hypothecate

To pledge a thing without delivering the possession of it to the pledgee, or to pledge to a creditor in security for some debt or demand, but without transfer of title or delivery of possession.

Insured Loan

A loan made by a private lender and insured by the government.

Interest Credit

The amount of interest the government will pay to make up the difference between the maximum allowable interest rate and what the borrower can afford to pay.

Interim Financing

A temporary loan covering the costs of land, building materials, current real estate taxes, and other incidental expenses incurred during the construction period. An interim or construction loan is usually obtained by the builder.

Land Contract

A contract for the purchase of real estate on an installment basis. Upon payment of the last installment, the deed is delivered to the buyer.

Leasehold

The estate held by virtue of a lease.

Lessee

A tenant under a lease.

Lessor

One who leases

Levy

To raise—for example, to levy or raise a tax or an assessment; or to seize—for example, to levy an execution to raise money for the payment of a judgment.

Lien

A hold or claim that one person has upon the property of another as a security for some debt or charge.

Loan-Closing Charges

Those charges that arise out of the final closing of a loan and the compliance with all the instructions of the mortgagor and mortgagee.

Locked Mortgage

A conventional loan on a security other than a home loan in which additional installment payments or full payoff of the loan is prohibited for a specified number of years.

Market Interest Rate (MIR)

The maximum amount of interest that can be charged on federally insured mortgages. For FmHA loans, the rate is determined at the start of that fiscal year by the Treasury Department and is based on a formula geared to what it costs the government to borrow. For FHA-insured loans, the rate is set periodically by the secretary of HUD and is geared to the prevailing rates of interest charged on conventional mortgages.

Mechanic's Lien

A claim, created by statutory law in most states, existing in favor of mechanics or other persons who have performed work or furnished materials in and for the erection or repair of a building. A mechanic's lien attaches to the land as well as to the building.

Mortgage

A contract by which specific property is hypothecated for the performance of an act without the necessity of a change of possessions.

Mortgage Insurance

A policy, usually taken on the head of the household, that will fulfill all mortgage commitments in the event he should become disabled or die.

Mortgage Insurance Premium

The price paid by the borrower for insurance under FHA loans, furnished by the federal government in favor of the lender, insuring payment of the loan in the event of default by the borrower after foreclosure.

Mortgage Market

The source of commercial credit for the purchase of mortgages. It usually refers to commercial investors, such as mortgage banks, insurance companies, and pension plans, which deal exclusively in commercial or residential construction. Financing generally runs to large project mortgages as opposed to individual mortgages.

Mortgage Paper

The security that the lender holds on the loan made to the borrower. The lender, particularly FmHA, often sells the mortgage paper on the open market to private investors, guaranteeing the mortgage will be paid off and guaranteeing a set return on the investment. Through this mechanism, the lender replenishes lending capital.

Mortgage Period

The length of time the borrower has to repay his housing loan. Mortgages generally have periods of at least 20 years. Mortgages under federally assisted programs are generally for 30 to 50 years.

Mortgage Terms

The conditions that the borrower must meet to fulfill his obligations.

Mortgagee

The lending party under the terms of a mortgage.

Mortgagor

The borrowing party that pledges property.

Option

The right, acquired for a consideration, to buy or sell something at a fixed price within a specific time.

Patent Deed

Conveyance of title to government land.

Plat

A map showing dimensions of a piece of real estate based upon the legal description.

Points

Charges made by a lending institution to increase its return on investment. In general, one point is equal to 1 percent of the loan and represents an added cost to the borrower. They are usually associated with federally insured mortgages, which carry a ceiling on allowable interest charges.

Repayment Penalty

Penalty for the payment of a debt before it actually becomes due.

Principal

The outstanding balance of a loan. Mortgage payments are separated into two parts—one goes to pay the interest on the loan and the other to reduce the principal.

Promissory Note

A note bearing evidence of debt and transferable by endorsement.

Quitclaim Deed

A deed of release. An instrument by which all right, title, or interest that one person has in or to an estate held by himself or another is released or relinquished to another.

Realtor

A real estate broker who is a member of the National Association of Real Estate Boards. He can be the official agent for either the buyer or the seller.

Reamortization

A method to allow a delinquent borrower to pay off what he is behind by spreading this amount over the balance of the mortgage period, thereby making his payments higher. Since FmHA is prohibited in most circumstances from refinancing loans, this is the method used to avoid foreclosure on a borrower.

Real Property

Land and, generally, whatever is erected on, growing upon, or affixed to land.

Refinancing

A method by which the original mortgage is paid off through issuing a new mortgage to either the original borrower or a new one. Refinancing is generally used to extend the mortgage period or to achieve more favorable interest terms.

Right of Way

Authority to use the lands of another for ingress and egress.

Security

The means by which the lender assures himself that his money is protected should the borrower default on the loan. The security on a car loan, for example, is generally the car itself. The security on housing loans is the housing, as secured by the mortgage.

Seed Money/Front Money

The amount of capital needed to get a project off the ground, usually recoverable in the mortgage loan. Items usually covered are the option agreement, partial payment of professional services, site surveys, FHA fees, and FNMA fees.

Site

The land or property to be developed for new construction or rehabilitation.

Special Assessment

A special charge against real estate, such as a street assessment or a sewer assessment, for installation of public improvements from which the property benefits.

Subordination

The act of a creditor acknowledging in writing that the debt due him from a debtor shall be inferior to the debt due another creditor from the same debtor.

Surety

One who is legally liable upon the default of another.

Title

The means whereby the owner of lands has the just possession of his property.

Title Binder

Temporary title insurance.

Title Insurance

A contract to reimburse the purchaser if he suffers any loss caused by encumbrances on your property. It is usually issued after a title opinion has been rendered. FmHA requires a title insurance policy on all rural housing loans.

Title Search (Abstract)

A method of checking the condition of the title to a piece of property by examination of official records dealing with transactions involving the property.

Trust Deed

An agreement in writing conveying property from the owner to a trustee for the accomplishment of the objectives set forth in the agreement. Trust deeds are generally used in many states rather than mortgages to secure loans on real property.

Trustee

A person, real or juristic, holding property in trust.

Waiver

The relinquishment of a right or the refusal to accept a right.

Warrant

A covenant whereby the grantor of an estate and his heirs are bound to warrant and defend the title.

Zoning

A legislative process by which restrictions are placed upon the use to which real property may be put.

HOUSING ACTION RESOURCES

American Association of Retired
Persons
1909 K Street, N.W.
Washington D.C. 20049

American Federation of Labor-
Congress of Industrial Organizations
815 16th Street, N.W.
Washington, D.C. 20006

American Friends Service Committee
1822 R Street, N.W.
Washington, D.C. 20009

American Jewish Committee's
National Job-Linked-Housing
Center
165 East 56th Street
New York, New York 10022

Anti-Defamation League of
B'nai B'rith
315 Lexington Avenue
New York, New York 10016

Birmingham Coalition
1880 Genesee
Toledo, Ohio 43605

Buckeye Community Congress
10613 Lamontier
Cleveland, Ohio 44104

Center for Community Change
1000 Wisconsin Ave., N.W.
Washington, D.C. 20007

Center for National Policy Review
620 Michigan Avenue, N.W.
Washington, D.C. 20017

Center for Study of Responsive
Law
P.O. Box 19367
Washington, D.C. 20036

Central Seattle Council Federation
2410 East Cherry
Seattle, Washington 98122

Citizen Advocate Center
1145 19th Street, N.W.
Washington, D.C. 20036

Department of Housing and Urban
Development (see p. 169)

Housing Assistance Council
1601 Connecticut Avenue, N.W.
Washington, D.C. 20009

Interreligious Coalition for Housing
Room 1268
475 Riverside Drive
New York, New York 10027

League of Women Voters
1730 M Street, N.W.
Washington, D.C. 20005

Metro Act
277 North Goodman
Rochester, New York 14607

Metropolitan Area Housing Alliance
121 West Superior
Chicago, Illinois 60610

Morris Heights Improvement
Association
1618 Grand
Bronx, New York 10453

National Association for the
Advancement of Colored People
10 Columbus Circle
New York, New York 10019

National Association for Community Development
1424 16th Street, N.W.
Washington, D.C. 20036

National Association of Home
Builders
15th and M Streets, N.W.
Washington, D.C. 20005

National Association of Housing
and Redevelopment Officials
2600 Virginia Avenue, N.W.
Washington, D.C. 20037

National Center for Housing
Management
1133 15th Street, N.W.
Washington, D.C. 20005

National Committee Against
Discrimination in Housing
1425 H Street, N.W.
Washington, D.C. 20005

National Conference of Catholic Charities
1346 Connecticut Avenue, N.W.
Suite 307
Washington, D.C. 20036

National Consumer Law Center
Boston College Law School
Brighton, Massachusetts 02135

National Council of Senior Citizens
1511 K Street, N.W.
Washington, D.C. 20036

National Council on the Aging
1828 L Street, N.W.
Washington, D.C. 20036

National Housing and Human Development Alliance
2 North Riverside Plaza
15th Floor
Chicago, Illinois 60606

National Housing Partnership
1133 15th Street, N.W.
Washington, D.C. 20005

National Housing Services
Valley Forge, Pennsylvania 19481

National Housing Training and
Information Center
121 West Superior
Chicago, Illinois 60610

National Neighbors
17 Maplewood Mall
Philadelphia, Pennsylvania 19144

National People's Action on Housing
121 West Superior
Chicago, Illinois 60610

National People's Caucus
1109 North Ashland Avenue
Chicago, Illinois 60622

National Rural Housing Coalition
1346 Connecticut Avenue, N.W.
Washington, D.C. 20036

National Tenants' Organization
1346 Connecticut Avenue, N.W.
Washington, D.C. 20036

National Urban League
55 East 52nd Street
New York, New York 10022

North Toledo Organizing
513 Magnolia
Toledo, Ohio 43604

Oakland Training Center
3914 East 14th
Oakland, California 94601

PACE
557 Public
Providence, Rhode Island 02907

Rural Housing Alliance
1346 Connecticut Avenue, N.W.
Washington, D.C. 20036

HOUSING NEWS

Your local newspapers

Congressional Record

Federal Register

Housing Affairs Letter
Community Development Services, Inc.
1319 F Street, N.W.
Washington, D.C. 20004

Housing and Development Reporter
Bureau of National Affairs, Inc.
1213 25th Street, N.W.
Washington, D.C. 20037

Housing and Urban Affairs Daily
National Housing Publications, Inc.
1182 National Press Building
Washington, D.C. 20004

Lawyers Title News
Lawyers Title Insurance Corporation
Box 27567
Richmond, Virginia 23261

Lutheran Housing Coalition Newsletter
955 L'Enfant Plaza
Washington, D.C. 20024

DIRECTORY OF DEPARTMENT OF
HOUSING AND URBAN DEVELOPMENT

Central Office

Department of Housing and Urban Development
451 7th Street, S.W.
Washington, D.C. 20410
(202) 755-5111

Region 1

Regional Office
Room 800
John F. Kennedy Federal Build-
  ing
Boston, Massachusetts 02203
(617) 223-4066

Area Offices

Bulfinch Building
15 New Chardon Street
Boston, Massachusetts 02114
(617) 223-4111

999 Asylum Avenue
Hartford, Connecticut 06105
(203) 244-3638

Davison Building
1230 Elm Street
Manchester, New Hampshire
  03101
(603) 669-7681

Insuring Offices

U.S. Federal Building & Post
  Office
202 Harlow Street
Bangor, Maine 04401
(207) 942-8341

330 Post Office Annex
Providence, Rhode Island 02903
(401) 528-4351

Room 630 Federal Building
Elmwood Avenue
Burlington, Vermont 05401
(802) 862-6274

Region 2

Regional Office
26 Federal Plaza
New York, New York 10007
(212) 264-8068

Area Offices

Grant Building   Parkade Building
560 Main Street   519 Federal Street
Buffalo, New York 14202   Camden, New Jersey 08103
(716) 842-3510   (609) 963-2301

Gateway Building   666 Fifth Avenue
No. 1 Raymond Plaza   New York, New York 10019
Newark, New Jersey 07102   (212) 974-6800
(201) 645-3010

GPO Box 3869
San Juan, Puerto Rico 00936
(8 202) 967-1221

Insuring Office

Westgate North
30 Russell Road
Albany, New York 12206
(518) 472-3567

Region 3

Regional Office
Curtis Building
6th and Walnut Streets
Philadelphia, Pennsylvania 19106
(215) 597-2560

Area Offices

Mercantile Bank & Trust Building
2 Hopkins Plaza
Baltimore, Maryland 21203
(301) 962-2121

Universal North Building
1875 Connecticut Avenue, N.W.
Washington, D.C. 20009
(202) 382-4855

701 E. Franklin Street
Richmond, Virginia 23219
(804) 782-2721

625 Walnut Street
Philadelphia, Pennsylvania 19106
(215) 597-2645

Two Allegheny Center
Pittsburgh, Pennsylvania 15212
(412) 644-2802

Insuring Offices

Farmers Bank Building
919 Market Street
14th Floor
Wilmington, Delaware 19801
(302) 571-6330

New Federal Building
500 Quarrier Street
Charleston, West Virginia 25301
(304) 343-1321

Region 4

Regional Office
1371 Peachtree Street, N.E.
Atlanta, Georgia 30309
(404) 526-5585

Area Offices

230 Peachtree Street, N.W.
Atlanta, Georgia 30303
(404) 526-4576

1801 Main Street Jefferson
  Square
Columbia, South Carolina 29202
(803) 795-5591

101 C Third Floor
Jackson Mall
300 Woodrow Wilson Avenue
Jackson, Mississippi 39213
(601) 969-4703

1 Northshore Building
1111 Northshore Drive
Knoxville, Tennessee 37919
(615) 524-1222

Daniel Building
15 S. 20th Street
Birmingham, Alabama 35233
(205) 325-3264

2309 Northwestern Plaza
W. Cone Boulevard
Greensboro, North Carolina
  27408
(919) 275-5361

Peninsula Plaza
661 Riverside Avenue
Jacksonville, Florida 32204
(904) 791-2626

Children's Hospital Foundation
  Building
601 S. Floyd Street
P.O. Box 1044
Louisville, Kentucky 40201
(502) 582-5251

Insuring Offices

3001 Ponce de Leon Boulevard
Coral Gables, Florida 33134
(305) 350-6221

U.S. Courthouse Federal Annex
  Building
801 Broadway
Nashville, Tennessee 37203
(615) 749-5521

100 N. Main Street
28th Floor
Memphis, Tennessee 38103
(901) 534-3141

4224 Henderson Boulevard
Tampa, Florida 33609
(813) 228-2501

Region 5

Regional Office
300 South Wacker Drive
Chicago, Illinois 60606
(312) 353-5680

Area Offices

1 North Dearborn Street
Chicago, Illinois 60602
(312) 353-7660

660 Woodward Avenue
First National Building
5th Floor
Detroit, Michigan 48226
(313) 226-7900

744 North Fourth Street
Milwaukee, Wisconsin 53203
(414) 224-1493

60 East Main Street
Columbus, Ohio 43215
(614) 469-7345

4720 Kingsway Drive
Indianapolis, Indiana 46205
(317) 269-6303

1821 University Avenue
St. Paul, Minnesota 55104
(612) 725-4701

Insuring Offices

550 Main Street
Room 9009
Cincinnati, Ohio 45202
(513) 684-2884

777 Rockwell Avenue
Cleveland, Ohio 44114
(216) 522-4065

2922 Fuller Avenue, N.E.
Grand Rapids, Michigan 49505
(616) 456-2225

524 South Second Street
Springfield, Illinois 62704
(217) 525-4414

Region 6

Regional Office
Federal Office Building
1100 Commerce Street
Dallas, Texas 75202
(214) 749-7401

Area Offices

2001 Bryan Tower
4th Floor
Dallas, Texas 75201
(214) 749-1601

Kallison Building
2nd Floor
410 S. Main Avenue
P.O. Box 9163
San Antonio, Texas 78285
(512) 225-4685

1 Union National Plaza
Little Rock, Arkansas 72201
(501) 378-5401

301 North Hudson Street
Oklahoma City, Oklahoma 73102
(405) 231-4891

Plaza Tower
1001 Howard Avenue
New Orleans, Louisiana 70113
(504) 589-2063

Insuring Offices

625 Truman Street, N.E.
Albuquerque, New Mexico 87110
(505) 843-3251

Two Greenway Plaza
Suite 200
Houston, Texas 77046
(713) 226-4335

New Federal Building
500 Fannin
6th Floor
Shreveport, Louisiana 71120
(318) 226-5385

Federal Building
819 Taylor Street
Room 13A 11
Fort Worth, Texas 76102
(817) 334-3233

Federal Building
1205 Texas Avenue
Lubbock, Texas 79401
(806) 762-7265

1708 Utica Square
P.O. Box 4054
Tulsa, Oklahoma 74152
(918) 581-7435

Region 7

Regional Office
Federal Office Building
911 Walnut Street
Room 300
Kansas City, Missouri 64106
(816) 374-2664

Area Offices

Two Gateway Center
4th and State Streets
P.O. Box 1339
Kansas City, Kansas 66117
(816) 374-4355

210 North 12th Street
St. Louis, Missouri 63101
(314) 425-4761

Univac Building
7100 West Center Road
Omaha, Nebraska 68106
(402) 221-9301

Insuring Offices

210 Walnut Street
Des Moines, Iowa 50309
(515) 284-4512

700 Kansas Avenue
Topeka, Kansas 66603
(913) 234-8241

Region 8

Regional Office
Federal Building
1961 Stout Street
Denver, Colorado 80202
(303) 837-4881

Insuring Offices

Title Building
4th Floor
909 17th Street
Denver, Colorado 80202
(303) 837-2441

Federal Building
653 2nd Avenue N.
P.O. Box 2483
Fargo, North Dakota 58102
(701) 237-5136

125 South State Street
Salt Lake City, Utah 84111
(801) 524-5237

616 Helena Avenue
Helena, Montana 59601
(406) 442-3237

Federal Building
400 S. Phillips Avenue
Sioux Falls, South Dakota 57102
(605) 336-2223

Federal Building
100 East B Street
P.O. Box 580
Casper, Wyoming 82601
(307) 265-3252

Region 9

Regional Office
450 Golden Gate Avenue
P.O. Box 36003
San Francisco, California 94102
(415) 556-4752

Area Offices

2500 Wilshire Boulevard
Los Angeles, California 90057
(213) 688-5973

1 Embarcadero Center
Suite 1600
San Francisco, California 94111
(415) 556-2238

Insuring Offices

244 West Osborn Road
P.O. Box 13468
Phoenix, Arizona 85002
(602) 261-4434

110 West C Street
P.O. Box 2648
San Diego, California 92112
(714) 293-5310

1000 Bishop Street
P.O. Box 3377
Honolulu, Hawaii 96813
(415) 556-0220 to reach "O" for
    546-2136

801 I Street
P.O. Box 1978
Sacramento, California 95809
(916) 449-3471

1440 East First Street   1050 Bible Way
Santa Ana, California 92701   P.O. Box 4700
(213) 836-2451   Reno, Nevada 89505
                                                (702) 784-5356

Region 10

Regional Office
3003 Arcade Plaza Building
1321 Second Avenue
Seattle, Washington 98101
(206) 442-5414

Area Offices

Cascade Building   Arcade Plaza Building
520 S.W. Sixth   1321 Second Avenue
Portland, Oregon 97204   Seattle, Washington 98101
(503) 221-2561   (206) 442-7456

Insuring Offices

334 West Fifth Avenue   331 Idaho Street
Anchorage, Alaska 99501   P.O. Box 32
(206) 442-0150 to reach "O" for   Boise, Idaho 83707
  265-4-871   (208) 342-2232

746 U.S. Courthouse
920 Riverside Avenue
Spokane, Washington 99201
(509) 456-2510

DIRECTORY OF STATE HOUSING AGENCIES

Alaska

Talbert E. Elliott,
  Executive Director
Alaska State Housing Finance
  Corp.
P.O. Box 80
Anchorage, Alaska 99510
(907) 274-4976

Colorado

Walter C. Kane,
  Executive Director
Colorado Housing Finance
  Authority
1115 Grant Street
Denver, Colorado 80203
(303) 861-8962

Connecticut

John Maylott,
  Executive Director
Connecticut Housing Finance
  Authority
1179 Main Street
Hartford, Connecticut 06101
(203) 525-9311

Delaware

Robert S. Moyer, Director
Delaware State Housing Authority
55 The Green
Dover, Delaware 19901
(302) 678-4264

Georgia

Keith A. Waldrop
Georgia Residential Finance
  Agency
142 State Capitol
Atlanta, Georgia 30334
(404) 656-6679

Hawaii

Yoshio Yanagawa,
  Executive Director
Hawaii Housing Authority
Department of Social Services
  and Housing
P.O. Box 17907
Honolulu, Hawaii 96817
(808) 845-6491

Idaho

Barbara Sall, Executive Director
Idaho State Housing Agency
P.O. Box 894
Boise, Idaho 83701
(208) 336-0161

Illinois

Irving M. Gerick, Director
Illinois Housing Development
  Authority
201 North Wells Street
Chicago, Illinois 60606
(312) 793-2060

Kentucky

John W. Polk, Jr.,
 Executive Director
Kentucky Housing Corporation
Department for Finance and Ad-
 ministration
1121 Louisville Road
Frankfort, Kentucky 40601
(502) 564-7630

Louisiana

Champ L. Baker, Chairman
Louisiana Development
 Authority for Housing Finance
c/o Kisatchie-Delta Economic
 Development District Council,
 Inc.
1254 Dorchester Drive
Alexandria, Louisiana 71301
(318) 445-9388

Maine

James E. Mitchell, Director
Maine State Housing Authority
128 Sewall Street
State House Complex
Augusta, Maine 04330
(207) 622-3126

Maryland

William Hunt, Director of Housing
Maryland Department of Economic and Community Development
2525 Riva Road
Annapolis, Maryland 21401
(301) 267-1176

Massachusetts

William J. White, Director
Massachusetts Housing Finance
 Agency
45 School Street
Boston, Massachusetts 02108
(617) 723-9770

Michigan

David L. Froh, Executive
 Director
Michigan State Housing Development Authority
300 South Capitol Avenue
Lansing, Michigan 48926
(517) 373-8370

Minnesota

James F. Dlugosch, Executive
 Director
Minnesota Housing Finance Agency
First Floor, Hanover Building
480 Cedar Street
St. Paul, Minnesota 55101
(612) 296-6959

Missouri

William R. Moore, Executive
 Director
Missouri Housing Development
 Commission
20 West 9th Street, Suite 934
Kansas City, Missouri 64105
(816) 421-1045

New Jersey

William L. Johnston, Executive
 Director
New Jersey Housing Finance Agen
101 Oakland Street
Trenton, New Jersey 08618
(609) 292-6447

Judd S. Levy, Deputy Director
New Jersey Mortgage Finance
  Agency
36 West State Street
Trenton, New Jersey 08625
(609) 292-5265

New York

John G. Burnett, Executive
  Vice-President
New York State Urban Development Corporation
1345 Avenue of the Americas
New York, New York 10019
(212) 974-7028

Lee Goodwin, Commissioner
New York State Division of Housing and Community Renewal
2 World Trade Center
New York, New York 10047
(212) 488-7126

Paul Belica, Executive
  Director
New York State Housing Finance
  Agency
1250 Broadway
New York, New York 10001
(212) 736-4949

Edward R. Levy, Executive
  Director
New York City Housing Development Authority
110 William Street
New York, New York 10038
(212) 962-4200

North Carolina

Harland E. Boyles, Deputy
  State Treasurer
North Carolina Housing Finance
  Agency
c/o Department of State Treasury
Albermarle Building
325 North Salisbury Street
Raleigh, North Carolina 27604
(919) 829-3064

Ohio

William A. Losoncy, Executive
  Director
Ohio Housing Development Board
34 North High Street
Columbus, Ohio 43215
(614) 466-7970

Oregon

M. Gregg Smith, Administrator
Housing Division
Oregon Department of Commerce
308 State Library Building
Salem, Oregon 97310
(503) 378-4343

Pennsylvania

John M. McCoy, Jr., Executive
  Director
Pennsylvania Housing Finance
  Agency
3211 North Front Street
Harrisburg, Pennsylvania 17110
(717) 787-1450

Rhode Island

Ralph Pari, Executive Director
Rhode Island Housing and Mortgage Finance Corporation
40 Westminister Street
Providence, Rhode Island 02903
(401) 751-5566

South Carolina

L. Steve Mayfield, Executive
  Director
South Carolina State Housing
  Authority
1122 Lady Street, Suite 1101
Columbia, South Carolina 29201
(803) 758-2844

South Dakota

Robert T. Hiatt, Executive
  Director
South Dakota Housing Development Authority
120 East Capitol Street
Pierre, South Dakota 57501
(605) 224-3181

Tennessee

Joseph H. Torrence, Executive
  Director
Tennessee Housing Development
  Agency
500 Hamilton Bank Building
Nashville, Tennessee 37219
(615) 741-1081

Vermont

Richard W. Lincoln, Executive
  Director
Vermont Housing Finance Agency
P.O. Box 408
Burlington, Vermont 05401
(802) 864-5743

Virginia

Kenneth G. Hance, Jr., Execu-
  tive Director
Virginia Housing Development
  Authority
Imperial Building
5th and Franklin Streets
Richmond, Virginia 23219
(804) 649-7041

West Virginia

Leonard A. Crosby, III, Executive Director
West Virginia Housing Development Fund
900 Charleston National Plaza
Charleston, West Virginia 25301
(304) 348-3732

Wisconsin

George D. Simos, Executive
  Director
Wisconsin Housing Finance
  Authority
14 North Carroll Street
Madison, Wisconsin 53702
(608) 266-7884

ALEXANDER GREENDALE, National Director of the American Jewish Committee's Housing Division and its National Job-Linked Housing Center (which is committed to developing strategies and programs to increase the housing supply for low-skilled and semiskilled workers near their jobs), shares the responsibility of developing and implementing the American Jewish Committee program in metropolitan areas. His major concentration is on intergroup relations as they affect housing. He is also responsible for providing guidelines and assistance to local AJC chapters in their work in this field.

A trained social worker with a B.A. from the University of Hawaii, an M.A. from Stanford University, and an M.S.S. from Adelphi University, Mr. Greendale has had extensive experience in working with low-, moderate-, and middle-income families. Prior to joining AJC's National Staff he was project specialist with the Community Service Society of New York, in which he directed a family life education and management training demonstration program sponsored jointly with the New York City Housing Authority. In the 1960s he was director of the Department of Community Work and Housing for the Lenox Hill Neighborhood Association. He has been a lecturer at the City College of New York, Barnard College, and the Adelphi University School of Social Work.

He has published The Kipling Sampler, Fawcett Publications, 1945, second edition, 1947; Life in Public Housing Equals Tenants Plus Management, Community Service Society of New York, 1971; Guidelines to Scatter Site Public Housing, American Jewish Committee, 1971; and Are New Towns for Lower Income Americans Too? coedited with John C. DeBoer, published by Praeger Publishers, 1974.

Before going into social work, Mr. Greendale was a dramatist. He had numerous productions, among them "Walk into My Parlor" produced on Broadway in 1941. He was the recipient of many major playwriting fellowships and awards, including the Rockefeller, Theater Guild, and Guggenheim Fellowships, and awards from the American Academy of Arts and Letters and the American National Theater and Academy.

STANLEY F. KNOCK, JR. is the Washington Representative of the United Methodist Church and the Interreligious Coalition for Housing. He has been a Minister of the United Methodist Church for 25 years. He is well-known for his Church-related research in Latin American and European countries.

Reverend Knock has a B.A. from Scarritt College; a B.D. from the Divinity School, Yale University; an M.A. from American University; and is a Ph.D. candidate, American University. He has been affiliated in a variety of capacities with the Religious Education Association, the National Association for Educational Broadcasters, and the Association for Educational Communication and Technology. He has written extensively on a variety of Church subjects for the past 25 years. He has won many honors and awards in the religious field.

RELATED TITLES
Published by
Praeger Special Studies

HOUSING MARKET PERFORMANCE IN THE
UNITED STATES
Charles J. Stokes
Ernest M. Fisher

HOUSING MARKETS AND CONGRESSIONAL GOALS
Ernest M. Fisher

THE POLITICS OF HOUSING IN OLDER URBAN
AREAS
edited by
Robert E. Mendelson
Michael A. Quinn

PROBLEM TENANTS IN PUBLIC HOUSING:
Who, Where, and Why Are They?
Richard S. Scobie

PUBLIC HOUSING AND URBAN RENEWAL: An
Analysis of Federal-Local Relations
Richard D. Bingham